the

beermat

entrepreneur

the
beermat
entrepreneur

turn your good idea into
a great business

Mike Southon and Chris West

an imprint of Pearson Education

London • New York • Toronto • Sydney • Tokyo • Singapore • Hong Kong • Cape Town
New Delhi • Madrid • Paris • Amsterdam • Munich • Milan • Stockholm

PEARSON EDUCATION LIMITED

Head Office:
Edinburgh Gate
Harlow CM20 2JE
Tel: +44 (0)1279 623623
Fax: +44 (0)1279 431059

London Office:
128 Long Acre
London WC2E 9AN
Tel: +44 (0)20 7447 2000
Fax: +44 (0)20 7240 5771
Website: www.business-minds.com
          www.yourmomentum.com

First published in Great Britain in 2002

© Pearson Education Limited 2002

The right of Mike Southon and Chris West to be identified as Authors
of this Work has been asserted by them in accordance
with the Copyright, Designs and Patents Act 1988.

ISBN 0 273 65929 4

British Library Cataloguing in Publication Data
A CIP catalogue record for this book can be obtained from the British Library

Library of Congress Cataloging in Publication Data Applied for.

10 9 8 7

Designed by Claire Brodmann Book Designs, Lichfield, Staffs
Illustrated by Bill Piggins and Robert Tuck.
Typeset by Northern Phototypesetting Co. Ltd, Bolton
Printed and bound in Great Britain by Bell & Bain Ltd, Glasgow

The Publishers' policy is to use paper manufactured from sustainable forests.

Contents

Note from Mike

Like great businesses, this book is a team effort. The entrepreneurial experience is mine, hence the pronoun 'I' used throughout a book apparently written by two people. Chris brought his outstanding literary and journalistic skills, plus his own business experience, to the party. Rachel Stock at Pearson turned our manuscript into a fine book – and most importantly shared our passion for its message as she did so.

It doesn't stop there, of course. Many people have looked at early drafts and given us the benefit of their knowledge and experience, which has enriched the end product enormously. Thanks to Bill Thompson, who came up with the book's title (we'd been pondering this for weeks; it took Bill about five minutes); to Martin Rich and Erik Larsen at City University Business School; to Robert Tuck of the mk group for his excellent beermat designs; to Scottish Courage for the use of the Foster's brand and their support for the project; to (in alphabetical order) David Baynes, John Beevor, Christine Comaford-Lynch, Nick Fleisiak, Sir Campbell Fraser, Rachael Gonzalez, Gervas Huxley, Sally Jones, Simon Linford, Ian Masson, Rick Medlock, Graham Michelli, Jamie Mitchell, Nick Moreno, Steve Packard, Dev Patel, Guy Reavley, Carol Sarler, Phil Tee and all the RiverSoftees, Peter Wallace, Chris Weller and Jim White.

Thanks also to everyone involved in The Instruction Set, both customers and employees, particularly the original beermat entrepreneur, Peter Griffiths, and the other cornerstones, David Griffiths, Mike Banahan and Andy Rutter. Without you, I would probably still be selling scaffolding...

A point on style. Our entrepreneur and team can be male or female. To use 'he' and 'his' all the time clearly fails to reflect this, but oscillating between 'he' and 'she' sounds silly, and endless repetitions of 'his or her' (or 'her or his') are just plain ugly. So we have mostly plumped for the 'singular they', e.g. 'The entrepreneur and their team...' Apologies to any purists. We also find the economists' mantra 'goods or services' rather ungainly, and prefer to talk of 'products'.

I'm always delighted to get comments from readers. Is there anything I have missed? What's *your* experience of founding and building a business? Can I help with any business problems? Please get in touch with me, mike@beermatentrepreneur.com, or visit the *Beermat Entrepreneur* website at www.beermatentrepreneur.com

Foreword

by Charles Dunstone,
Founder, The Carphone Warehouse

Entrepreneurs are great people, but they need all the help they can get. They also need both passion and clarity, this book provides both.

Entrepreneurs also need great people around them, and *The Beermat Entrepreneur* is particularly strong on the kind of people you need at the different stages of your business growth. First among these is a mentor: an idea that we also believe in at The Prince's Trust, where we connect businesses with seasoned professionals to provide advice, contacts and moral support. When I started Carphone Warehouse, I was lucky enough to receive excellent mentoring, and it made a huge difference.

This is not another book on theory; it is based on the authors' real life experiences at the sharp end. There is a great deal of wisdom in this book – enjoy it and learn from it. I recommend it to any aspiring entrepreneur.

Charles Dunstone is a member of The Prince's Trust Council
and Chairman of the Prince's Trust Trading Limited

Introduction

Once upon a time there were three people sitting in a pub.

These three people talked, as all people in pubs should do, about what they liked. Two tables away, a group of lads were talking about football. Next to us, an old couple were discussing gardening. We were talking about business.

One of us had this brilliant idea – he was always having brilliant ideas. But for once, his idea sounded special. Maybe this *would* work... I got another round in, and we began to look at the idea more closely, making notes on beermats as we had no paper to hand.

Five years later, our business, The Instruction Set, was employing more than 150 people. Soon after that, the company was sold, and we were millionaires.

After my earn-out period, I retired. Six months later, I started another business. It wasn't a 'failure', but it never really flew. Right now, I'm delighted it didn't, as I learned almost as much from its shortcomings as I did from my success. I then joined another entrepreneurial team, to help build a software company, which is now worth over $1 billion. No, I didn't get any stock options, but it was fun. Later I spent a year in a launch network for small companies, looking at hundreds of business plans and talking with their authors about practical ways of turning their neat ideas into real commercial enterprises.

And now I'm writing a book.

At the time of writing, the air is still clearing from the great dot-com collapse. Incredible amounts of money have been lost – because people have gone about founding businesses the wrong way. They have used the wrong people; they have had ridiculous faith in untested ideas; they have made the fundamental mistake of all bad business, that of not listening to the market (the real market of customers, not the fantasy world of stock and derivatives markets).

I don't want future entrepreneurs and their teams to make the same mistakes. I know how much work goes into setting up a business, and I don't want to see that effort wasted – as it will be if people continue to follow the 'dot-com boom' model of business.

HIGHWAY TO HELL:

The dotcom model of business development

➡ Get someone to come up with a clever-sounding idea

➡ Get some MBAs to invent a scenario whereby this idea makes pots of money

➡ Get a VC to throw millions of pounds at it

➡ Headhunt any skills you suddenly find you need (sales, accountants etc.)

➡ Get the hell out as quickly as possible, via an IPO

Please don't do any of this.

Let me tell you how to really make a business grow.

Business is easy

I know that will annoy a lot of people, but I really do believe it to be true. Almost all the business balls-ups I have seen – and I've seen plenty – have been due to people getting very simple things wrong.

Of course, success in business involves *hard work*. Lots of it, twenty-hours-a-day-for-five-years hard work. But if you love business, you're up for that. With the right people and the right motivation, you'll enjoy it most of the time (not *all* the time – business is not that easy).

Of course, success in business involves hard work. Lots of it, twenty-hours-a-day-for-five-years hard work.

Note the caveat 'if you love business'. If you don't get a buzz from business – the ideas, the technology, the people – you really shouldn't go near a start-up. Or any commercial organization, really. Scale down your financial ambitions and find another way of making a living and (as important) of making a difference to the world.

Business also involves making *hard choices* – not often, but occasionally. However, these choices are usually not as hard as they look. You usually know in your heart what you have to do; it's just a matter of summoning up the willpower.

Success also requires a measure of *luck*, but as the golfer Gary Player said: 'The harder I practise, the luckier I get.'

Most of all, though, I believe that success in business means *following the right pattern*. This is what this book is about: a pattern that begins with self-examination and grows naturally from there, potentially to a point where you are leading an organization that affects the lives of thousands of people: customers, employees, shareholders...

A successful business is a living thing. So like all living things, it has a natural pattern of growth. You ignore this pattern at your peril, just as if you fail to re-pot seedlings at the right time they'll die, or if you plant a sapling in the wrong kind of soil you'll soon be confronted with a dead-looking stick instead of that riot of colour that you saw at the garden centre.

Some people balk at this talk of patterns. Isn't business about flair and imagination? Isn't business an art as much as a science? The great entrepreneurs didn't sit around studying theory, any more than Monet and Rembrandt went out and bought those kits where you dab paint into little numbered sections.

I can only say that the more I see businesses fail or succeed, the more I believe that there is a pattern to their growth that has to be worked with to ensure success, and that I understand this pattern well enough to start telling other people about it.

There is, perhaps, an analogy with the way that scriptwriting is taught in Hollywood. There are strict rules for developing plots, rules which compel attention and make stories work. But they do not of themselves guarantee success: if they are followed without flair, the results are leaden (though still adequate – video rental places are full of them). You need aptitude *as well as* rules to excel.

Which is why you must begin your journey to business success by asking...

Where do I fit in?

The popular vision of a growing company is of a group of followers flocking round the banner of a charismatic entrepreneur/leader. The reality is much more subtle than this. Yes, there will no doubt be a classic Branson/Roddick figure at the centre of things, but they are not the whole story. Or even half of it. There are concentric rings of very special people around every entrepreneur without whom the business will go nowhere, without whom the entrepreneur will just spend their days dreaming or impressing people in pubs.

This book is for entrepreneurs, but also for the people who form these concentric rings, who are *just as important* as entrepreneurs. These people are not – and this is where many businesses go wrong – passive sidekicks but key players in their own right.

For any individual wanting to work in an entrepreneurial environment, the first question must be: 'What role am I best suited to play?'

The entrepreneur...

Entrepreneurs are, for all their faults (see below), very special people. Are you one? Look in this mirror and be honest: is the face staring back yours?

Entrepreneurs are *confident*. They're born optimists; they simply *know* they can do it. This optimism is often irrational – it can infuriate their more realistic friends – but it just bubbles up in them. 'I can do it!' And they *will* do it as well. It's not that they don't feel fear – all sane people do – but when push comes to shove, their confidence just steamrollers over the fear and they get on with what needs to be done.

Entrepreneurs are also *charismatic*. They inspire people. They're not just optimistic, they have optimism to spare, optimism which they radiate and instil into others around them. No wonder they attract people, not just sheep but energetic, imaginative winners. They'll need this quality, over and over again – with their business partners, with their employees, with their sources of finance, and most importantly of

Entrepreneurs are **confident.** They're born

optimists;

they simply know they can do it.

all with their customers. But that's fine, as they've got a seemingly endless supply of it.

I've seen a few apparent exceptions to this, but on closer examination, entrepreneurs all have charisma in the right circumstances. Bill Gates, for example, seems to lack this quality – to the general public. But I saw him years ago among a group of techies, and the man was a magnet.

Entrepreneurs have bags of *energy*. They're going to need it, every ounce of it. But somehow, they know it's there. All the entrepreneurs I have met seem to sleep less than normal.

Entrepreneurs are *obsessed with work*. They talk about it all the time. Not the best thing at parties, but it does make for success.

Entrepreneurs are *ambitious*. Obvious, you might say, but it's an essential part of the make-up. Ambition on its own, however, does not make an entrepreneur. A generalized ambition – 'I want to be rich' – isn't enough either. The entrepreneur's ambition is about *wanting to change things* and about knowing they have the wherewithal to make this change. What they change can be anything, from how clothes are sourced to a highly technical software application. Whatever, it sucks at the moment, and the entrepreneur is going to change it.

Entrepreneurs are *in a hurry*. Not only are they going to change things, they are going to change things fast.

Does this look like you? Great.

Now for the difficult bit.

Entrepreneurs are also *arrogant*. They know they are good. At everything. With a strong team around them – and they can't flourish without such a team – this attitude mellows to 'I'm good at everything.

But I don't have the time to do everything, so I have to let the people in finance, sales, delivery and so on get on with it'. But even then, the team need to remain on guard against the entrepreneur's passion for meddling. The worst thing about this meddling is that it is appallingly inconsistent. One day the entrepreneur will be stomping round the office fixing light bulbs, the next phoning up customers out of the blue, the next trying to rewrite software, the next...

This arrogance is the flip side of the entrepreneur's confidence and vision. Vision is not always a good trait: Hitler and Stalin 'knew they were right'. But then so did Winston Churchill and Mother Theresa.

Entrepreneurs are also *manipulative*. Just as arrogance is the flip side of the entrepreneur's confidence and vision, manipulation is the dark side of charisma. Entrepreneurs use people. They may inspire them, they may pay them well, they may enable them to achieve things they'd never achieve on their own – but they still use people.

Entrepreneurs *can't complete things*. They're forever coming up with new ideas. They love brainstorming sessions; they blaze with excitement at new projects. 'Why don't we...' 'Supposing...' 'And then we can...'

This inability to complete things is perhaps part of a bigger weakness, *lack of focus*. I said that entrepreneurs are obsessed with work, and they are. Yet at the same time they seem unable to focus on specific issues for any length of time. It's as if, having walled themselves away from most of what the rest of us call life, they have to pace round and round this little courtyard with extra energy. If you are an entrepreneur, please make yourself focus on detail. More important, listen to your closest colleagues when *they* focus on detail.

Entrepreneurs can become *obsessed with the competition*. I actually know one who founded a company with the sole purpose of putting a rival

If you are an entrepreneur, please make yourself focus on **detail.** More important, **listen** to your closest colleagues when they focus on detail.

out of business. I shall talk about 'how to compete' later, but I don't think I'm giving too much away by saying this obsession can be disastrous, both commercially and personally. If you feel yourself going down this road – don't. Concentrate on improving *your* proposition. 'I've got mine, don't worry 'bout his', as famed management guru James Brown puts it.

Entrepreneurs can be *impatient*. Throughout this book, I talk about the 'hurdles' that an idea has to jump in order to succeed. They are all listed in the back of the book (page 141), and each time a new hurdle is reached in the text, it will be flagged up by a hurdle icon in the margin. You can't miss these out and charge straight for the finishing line.

So there we have it. Mature, sophisticated, gentle? No. Childish, obsessive, ruthless – that's more like it. More like you?

I don't want to end this section on a negative note. Successful entrepreneurs create employment, opportunities, choice, wealth. They inspire people to do things of which they hardly imagined themselves capable. They challenge orthodoxy and they change society much more than most politicians ever do. If it weren't for these men and women of vision, with all their weaknesses, we'd probably still be sitting around in caves.

Entrepreneurs truly change the world.

But they don't do so alone.

...and their teams

It's clear from the above that the lone entrepreneur is not going to found, let alone run, a successful business. They'll lose interest too soon; they'll miss crucial details; they'll alienate key stakeholders – they'll be back in the pub again in no time, drawing another idea on another beermat.

They need a team around them.

Actually, they need two teams, a 'founding' team and a 'dream' team. These build at different stages of the business's growth. In its first stage, when the enterprise is still a seedling, the entrepreneur will need a group of four people around them. Four cornerstones, on which the business will be built. Later, when the enterprise grows to a sapling, 15 more people will be required: lively, passionate, committed team players like the sporting 'dream team'.

The four cornerstones

The engine room – and often the totality – of a start-up company is the entrepreneur, plus their four closest associates, the four cornerstones. The image that comes to mind is of a pyramid, with the entrepreneur at the apex and four rock-solid supports beneath them.

I shall talk about what the cornerstones actually *do* later. At the moment, I am concerned with what *sort* of people they are. The answer is a very special mixture of solidity and entrepreneurial passion.

Their *solidity* comes from their commercial or technical discipline. Cornerstones are professionals, at sales, accounts or management, or they are experts in the relevant technology. This expertise and professionalism provides essential objectivity. Objectivity is something entrepreneurs need badly, though they are usually in blissful ignorance of that need.

At the same time, cornerstones are not there just to pour cold water over the entrepreneur. They are nearly as *passionate* about the venture as the

Cornerstones

nearly as *passionate* about the venture as the entrepreneur is.

entrepreneur is. Sometimes, when the entrepreneur is in a sulk because some part of their dream isn't working out, the cornerstones are more passionate. But they never lose their objectivity, their priceless gift of perspective.

Cornerstones also have considerable *personal skills*. It's not enough just to be passionate about the idea and good at a business discipline. Working with the mercurial entrepreneur, cornerstones need to be able to tell the truth tactfully and to remain calm and cool when the entrepreneur still tries to overrule them.

They need the entrepreneur's capacity for *hard work* – there are no free rides in a new business.

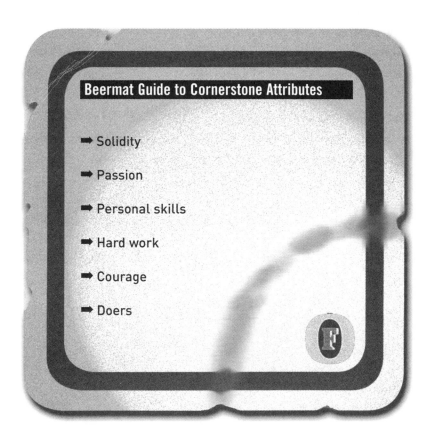

Beermat Guide to Cornerstone Attributes

➡ Solidity

➡ Passion

➡ Personal skills

➡ Hard work

➡ Courage

➡ Doers

They also need *courage*, probably more courage than the entrepreneur even, as entrepreneurs are driven by their vision, while cornerstones can see the potential hazards much more clearly.

Finally, cornerstones are *doers* – you give them a job and they get it done, whatever the obstacles.

There's one of those acronyms here. What you need in a cornerstone is lots of SPPHCD!

I hate acronyms.

The cornerstones' qualities will make the difference between the new company's success and failure. They will do so when the company is tiny; they will do so later, when the cornerstones bring these skills to bear in managing not only the entrepreneur but also a growing number of subordinates.

The dream team

When the business expands further, a wider set of supports will be needed. I talk about this 'dream team' in the chapter on the sapling enterprise. This second, outer ring of people is still very special. Like

The entrepreneur and their teams

cornerstones, they are a mixture of solid commercial/technical skill and entrepreneurial flair. Probably the main difference between them and the cornerstones is their level of skill, which will be a little lower. They will be passionate and imaginative and above all team players, hence the allusion to 'dream teams' in sport.

The intrapreneur

Do you work for a big company but secretly dream of being an entrepreneur? Do you at the same time fear the loss of security that would come from packing in the job and 'going it alone'? I have met plenty of people in this situation.

The way forward is to become an 'intrapreneur', to set up (or join) an entrepreneurial division within your company. As the marketplace becomes ever more competitive and fast-moving, more and more businesses are setting up such divisions. They are right to be doing so, and if your employer is not, you could be doing them, and yourself, a big favour by getting them onto this bandwagon.

The classic model of the enterprise division is the Apple 'skunkworks', complete with Jolly Roger over its outbuildings. They saved the company, which was throwing money at an overspecified machine called the Lisa, by developing the Macintosh. The boss of the skunkworks, Steve Jobs, then left the company, which began to drift again. Only when he returned, hoisted the skull and crossbones once more and came up with products like the iMac, did Apple begin to flourish again.

The story of the Post-It note, developed inside the 3M company by Arthur Fry, is another classic. Fed up with page markers that kept falling out of his hymn book, Fry developed a marker backed with a 'failed' experimental glue – a glue that had been rejected because of its low sticking power. He presented the idea to his superiors, who politely

Intrapreneurism
is not
a soft option.

sidelined it. He made some prototypes and gave them to the secretaries in his office, who soon found them indispensable. The bosses noticed...

In both the above stories, the 'intrapreneur' had to fight hard for their product against a sceptical corporate bureaucracy, and this is often the case. Intrapreneurism is not a soft option.

However, it does have some advantages over the traditional start-up. The mother company can provide things such as premises, funding and contacts that the entrepreneur has to fight for. But the fundamental process of building an enterprise is the same within a company as outside it, so intrapreneurs should read this book and follow it as closely as entrepreneurs in the wicked world out there.

Note that for companies, letting intrapreneurs loose is not a 'pure win' – there will be some downside. Remember those negative attributes of entrepreneurs: you are just about to unleash these people on your nice corporate culture. Some valuable, solid team players may be offended by their unconventional attitudes and buccaneering style. Of course, I think you've done the right thing – you're getting back to being a proper business again, not a Jurassic bureaucracy. But watch out for a few internal bruises.

Private life: a warning

Setting up and running a business is about as demanding an activity as you can get. If you are in a relationship, it may not survive the competition. If you already have a family, think very carefully about how you are going to balance out your time.

Entrepreneurs and cornerstones often tell their long-suffering partners: 'I'm doing this to make us rich.' This is at best a half-truth. You're doing this because you need to, somewhere deep within you. Money is only a part of the reward. Some partners may resent this: 'You have me, why do you need this business as well?' Talk these issues through.

If you have kids, the issue gets more serious still. I'm not saying don't start a business – and if I did, and you were a natural entrepreneur, you wouldn't listen anyway – but work this out. Talk to your partner.

You can forget that much-loved hobby, of course.

So you've done this, and you're ready to go. And you were honest about yourself and so really know what role suits you best. Entrepreneur? Cornerstone? Dream-team player? Intrapreneur?

The adventure starts here.

the

seedling

enterprise

There are three essential stages that a business passes through on its way to maturity. These stages are radically different to one another – in culture, in people, in management style, in finance, in selling... In everything, really.

So different and distinct are these stages that I nearly chose the image of a butterfly, whose larval, pupal and free-flying phases are totally unrecognizable as being of the same creature. But there is a little more continuity than this, and anyway, will the massive company you eventually build really resemble one of those beautiful but evanescent creatures that flaps across your garden on a summer's day (till the cat attacks it)? I prefer the image of an oak: mighty, spreading, long-lasting.

But your oak is a long way away yet. Right now, all we have is a simple acorn.

A good idea

I began my story in a pub, where an entrepreneur was coming up with ideas and two friends were listening... The trouble with that situation is that it happens too often: entrepreneurs are forever bubbling over with ideas. What you need is not ideas but *good* ideas, ones that really will grow into thriving businesses.

What you **need** is not ideas

but **good** ideas,

ones that really will grow into

thriving businesses.

Where do the really good ideas come from, and how do you know them when they crop up?

Where do they come from? In my view, the answer is personal experience.

A salesperson knows their customers have been crying out for a widget that does x, but nobody's making one at the moment. A technical expert is convinced that there's a way to write software that does y (or that does good old z much cheaper). An academic does original research, driving technology into new areas.

Yes, occasionally someone will emerge out of nowhere and overturn things radically. Thomas Edison is the classic example of this kind of inventor/entrepreneur, James Dyson a modern example. But most changes begin within an industry or technology.

Also, great business ideas often centre on a market dislocation. I define a *dislocation* as a change that radically alters the way people do things.

In other words, not 'the same thing but a bit better' but a totally new practice. In reality, the dividing line between improvement and dislocation is fuzzy. Clearly the latest 'improved' version of a washing powder lies one side of this line, and a totally new sociological phenomenon like the internet lies the other. In the middle? I would put Dyson's vacuum cleaner on the dislocation side, because it means people no longer have to buy bags – not exactly a massive sociological upheaval, yet a small but real change. By contrast, Dyson's new washing machine, though it also involves revolutionary technology, will probably not change the way people do things: it does an existing task better, so I'd put that on the 'improvement' side.

It is one of the joys of market dislocations that they tend to come from leftfield. Futurologists, City analysts and so on are busy at (and highly paid for) predicting market changes, and they almost always get it wrong. Who was it at IBM who said of the first computer that it was an interesting machine but there would probably be a market for only six of them? Or what about the talent scout at Decca Records who listened to The Beatles' demo and said that the days of groups with guitars were over? And as for the analysts, on Wall Street and elsewhere, who put those ridiculous valuations on unproven businesses...

Text messaging is the latest idea suddenly to catch on. The experts in the telecom business said it would replace pagers, which it has yet to do. They did not predict it would change the way teenagers communicate, which it has done, creating a whole new market for associated products like 'bks on txt msgs' and downloadable ring tones.

The relevance of this notion to the entrepreneur is that they should be keeping a very keen lookout for these dislocations. Note that you do not have to *cause* the dislocations. Yes, Dyson's cleaner did, but most entrepreneurs ride piggyback on dislocations – and thrive. Even a vast company like Cisco is still only a beneficiary of the internet dislocation, not its cause. *You don't have to instigate total, radical change to build an entrepreneurial business.* What you do need is to have a sharp eye for how things are going, especially when customer needs or behaviour are changing fast, and a real ability to make products to suit that change. 'In the future, there's going to be a real need for x's, and this is how we will deliver them.'

But back to our beermat entrepreneur and their mates in the pub...

How do you spot the winner? The answer to this, sadly, is 'you can't'. You only know the true mettle of an idea once you test it.

There are, however, a number of clear hurdles an idea has to jump. The first one is simply there, in the pub. If the entrepreneur's friends light up and someone says, 'Now that *is* a brilliant idea!', you have a small but real confirmation. Intuition is at work.

A second hurdle is next morning, when you wake up. In the clear light of day – and of sobriety – is it really such a good idea?

You don't have to

instigate

total, radical change

to build

an entrepreneurial business.

You should have decided the night before to go away and do a little research on the idea. If you are potential cornerstones, you will do this, not because you read it in my book but because your curiosity and professional pride will make you do so anyway. If you're in sales, you'll float the idea across customers, not trumpeting it from the rooftops but as an aside. If you're a techie, you'll knock up a prototype. If your forte is more delivery, you'll notice an ad in the paper offering cheap factory space.

 Gather again and compare notes. Are you still excited? Great. A third hurdle has been cleared.

 Now is the time to draw up your 'Beermat Plan'. Unlike the business plans beloved of MBAs, this plan is simple. It has three things on it:

1 Elevator Pitch
2 Mentor
3 First Customer

Your elevator pitch

Actually, the Beermat Plan contains half your elevator pitch. For those unfamiliar with the term, the elevator pitch is what you would say to Bill Gates if you found yourself in an elevator with him (or in a lift, if you meet Bill in the UK). I've heard hundreds of so-called elevator pitches, some lasting several hours! The perfect elevator pitch, by contrast, is only two sentences long: the *premise* and the *endorsement*.

At the moment your idea has no endorsement, so work on the premise – a one-sentence description of your product's unique benefits. 'Clothes with a conscience' made in safe factories by people paid fair wages. Friction-free widgets. A new kind of screen for 3G mobile phones. Dedicated software for market-gardeners…

This premise should become a mantra for the people in your organization; the automatic, and natural-sounding, answer when anyone asks what the company does. So now agree on a sentence that sums up the unique benefits the idea will bring its customers.

Note that the idea is still only a fraction of the way along its 'obstacle course'. It doesn't have to be perfect here, just still good enough. It will grow and change as you develop it, especially once you start talking to potential (and later, actual) customers.

Your mentor

Mentoring gets a passing mention in some of the books on entrepreneurial practice, but I believe it is a real key to success. Hewlett-Packard famously started in a garage: it probably would have stayed there if it hadn't been for the mentorship of Fred Terman, founder of Stanford Research Park. Among more recent successes, Hotmail and Carphone Warehouse both owe a great deal to good mentoring.

Now you're over that third hurdle, the next thing you must do is find a mentor. You are looking for someone with huge experience of business, who gets the point of what you're doing, who likes you and whom you like.

I'll expand on these 'qualifications' below, but right now I expect you are already imagining objections. I did when I first heard people talking about mentorship, but in retrospect my objections were all wrong. You're in the pub: what do people say to this idea?

⟹ 'Impossible. We don't know anyone like that.'

The second part of this objection may well be true. One of the aims of this book is to map out a path to success for people with an entrepreneurial mindset, whatever their current status or background. So maybe you're sitting here, now, and none of you knows anyone who falls into the category of potential mentor, or anybody remotely like that.

Relax. Finding a mentor is not impossible; it is simply a matter of will. If you make it a priority, and I'm saying that you *must* make it a priority, then you can find a mentor. In the process you will learn a lesson, which will prove of use again and again in all phases of business: the importance of making and pursuing priorities.

Of course it's easier to find a mentor if you're incredibly posh. Next time daddy has the chairman of BP over to dinner… But I certainly didn't have that advantage, and nor do most successful business-builders.

If you work in a particular industry you should have some idea of who the 'elders' of that industry are. If not, get such an idea, fast. Maybe you have met one or some of these people in the course of your work. So approach them. True 'elders' are usually happy to be approached by genuinely enthusiastic people with genuinely decent ideas.

If there is nobody in your sector, try adjacent business sectors. The qualities for mentorship do not include 'works in your sector': at the

True 'elders' are usually **happy** to be approached by **genuinely enthusiastic** people with genuinely **decent** ideas.

highest level, skill, thinking and contacts range across all types of business.

If you are starting from a very low base in terms of your current work – unemployed or very junior – it is harder to find a mentor of requisite quality. But not impossible. Set about your search slowly, systematically, imaginatively. All communities have leaders of various kinds. Who runs the Chamber of Commerce in your town? Your local religious leader may have a wealth of contacts you didn't know about. Check out institutions such as The Prince's Trust, which has an excellent mentoring system (see Appendix C), or your local Business Link. Ask yourself, 'Among people I can talk to, who do I respect the most?'

Students have no excuse for not finding a mentor. Your tutor should know people, or get an interview with your vice-chancellor, who, if they care about their post (and most of them do), will be delighted to help enterprise within 'their' college or university.

In passing, if you are a student (or fresh out of school and raring to get your business moving), it might be an idea to spend a couple of years in the business you intend to shake up so radically, not to have the radicalism knocked out of you, but to hone and temper it. Watch what people do: there'll be some good stuff you didn't know about. Make contacts. Start looking for potential cornerstones. Get closer to the movers and shakers in the industry. Give yourself a yardstick for when you run your own business (even if it's 'we're so much better than those people I worked for at ABC'). And, of course, let someone else pay the bill while you make early mistakes.

'First-step' people (local religious leader, college tutor) will not be mentors themselves, but they will know people who might be, or who (in turn) know people who might be. If you approach these people with seriousness and enthusiasm, they will move you towards the right person.

If you are *still* stuck for ideas, think of who has written a business book you really admire. Or think of a business you really admire, and find out who the directors are. A hint here is to avoid the obvious names – Richard Branson probably gets hundreds of ideas fired at him every day, but there are plenty of potentially superb mentors on boards of great companies for whom the experience would be refreshing.

➡ **'I don't want to deal with a load of old farts.'**

Someone will say that. Someone who's quite fun but a bit immature, probably. It's time they grew up and started taking people of all ages for what they are. The adventure of business success challenges everybody's preconceptions – class, sex, age, race. That's one of the purposes of pursuing it.

➡ **'Supposing they nick the idea?'**

This is an understandable fear, but grossly overrated. When I worked at the launch network, almost all the entrepreneurs I met wanted me to sign a non-disclosure agreement before they would let me read their business plan. I used to explain that success is about having a good idea *and putting it into practice*. Even the cleverest ideas are ten-a-penny. (It was company policy not to sign such agreements anyway, on the basis of our professional integrity.)

Once your idea is up and running and making money, then people will try to copy it. But don't worry about that now (or ever, really – see later). People who've made it to the top know this. They are also people who enjoy the business of putting ideas into practice. If they like your idea, they'll be excited by the prospect of helping you make it work, not by the prospect of pinching it.

➡ **'People like that won't listen to us.'**

'People at the top of businesses are bastards. They have to be, to get and stay there. They won't want to waste their time listening to wannabes.'

That's an urban myth.

Most top people are nice...

they have to be to get

people to work

for them.

Clearly there are a few very unpleasant people at the top of businesses – sadly some of them are entrepreneurs – but most of the top people I have met, and I've met lots, have been very nice. This is largely because they have to be, in order to get and keep good people to work for and with them.

'OK – but I don't know what to say to someone that important.'

Be yourself. Remember, you have a common passion with this person – business.

Don't expect Sir Everard Polymath to pick up the phone when you call, of course. Top people surround themselves with 'firewalls', people trained to filter out timewasters. Your first job is to persuade this 'firewall' that you are not a timewaster. This is not as hard as it may sound, as you are not a timewaster. And remember that the firewall is there not just to get rid of wasters but to facilitate welcome callers. Begin by finding out who Sir Everard's PA is. Then send them a simple e-mail, explaining who you are, that you want five minutes of *their* (not their boss's) time, and asking them to suggest a time that would be convenient for you to call. If you get no reply, call them and leave a voicemail to this effect.

When you do speak to the firewall, say that you want to speak to Sir Everard because you believe you have a business idea that would interest him. Tell them what the idea is (the premise of your elevator pitch). Add that you have the nucleus of the right team to make it work (the equivalent of the elevator pitch's endorsement). Explain why you chose Sir Everard (recommendation of college vice-chancellor, loved his book, really admired the way he's restructured Megacorp's food division). Don't bullshit here. It'll show and you will look ridiculous. If you are sincere, that will shine through too.

A good PA will either set up a brief conversation or say no and explain why. It may be that you have not expressed yourself quite clearly enough, which gives you the opportunity to restate your pitch. Or

A mentor is worth their weight in gold. They can be the difference between an idea's success and failure.

maybe Sir Everard is not interested in mentoring, in which case thank the PA politely and ask whether they know of anyone in their organization who would be interested. If the PA is rude, that's a sign that their boss was not for you, anyway. The kind of people who make good mentors employ polite, intelligent PAs, not human rottweilers.

If the idea of making these calls still fills you with horror, were you really honest when you looked at the profile of the entrepreneur and said 'that's me'? True entrepreneurs would enjoy this process. Or they would be so passionate about their idea that they wouldn't give these sorts of worries a second thought. Maybe you are better suited to being a cornerstone? Or, if you really do feel that, despite this evidence to the contrary, you are an entrepreneur by nature, you must find a sales cornerstone who has what it takes to make these calls.

Incidentally, though the entrepreneur needs chutzpah, this shouldn't be taken too far. In the film *Wall Street*, the Charlie Sheen character hounds Gordon Gekko mercilessly until the big guy takes him on. This is very Hollywood, and most British and European business people would be alienated by this. Most real, non-celluloid Americans would, too.

➡ **'Can't we just skip this stage and get on with it?'**

No. A mentor is worth their weight in gold. They can be the difference between an idea's success and failure. Remember that the qualities you will use and develop in the search for your mentor – courage, single-mindedness, sincerity – will be of enormous use in business later on, in dealing with colleagues and with the most important people in the universe, customers.

So go off and buy another round of drinks. Let the doubters have their say, then get on with finding a mentor.

No excuses.

What qualities must a mentor have?

Experience. The more the better. Forty years? Perfect. If you're in IT in any way, don't be an e-snob. The world doesn't divide into dudes or dinosaurs. I discovered the true value of mentoring when I worked for RiverSoft. Soon after joining, I turned up at work one morning to find a white-haired old man sitting in the chairman's office. I actually wondered if this was somebody's dad who'd come up to London for the day and was just sitting in an empty office, until I was told this was Sir Campbell Fraser, former chairman of Dunlop, Tandem and Scottish Television, and president of the Confederation of British Industry from 1982 to 1984. His role? Mentor to the company. Since that encounter I have found Sir Campbell to be the best source of business advice I have ever met. He has seen all kinds of business in all kinds of areas and understands the basic unchanging principles both of commerce and of human nature.

The mentor must '*get your idea*'. In a perfect world, they would react to it with the same excitement as the entrepreneur's mates did in the pub. But they're older and wiser, so they will be much more considered. If they like you and the idea, they'll go away and assess the assumptions and logic behind it.

If they don't like the idea, don't bin it at once. Try several other people. And never fob yourself off with someone big who 'quite likes' the idea. As every salesperson knows, 'maybe' is the worst possible answer. A clear 'no' sets you free to look elsewhere; an enthusiastic 'yes' means you're in business. 'Close' properly with your mentor: you are going to ask a lot of them and they will deliver only if their belief is real.

They must like you. How do you know? You just have to use your intuition here. You have a lot to offer them in terms of enthusiasm and liveliness, so offer it and watch them respond. Remember that they won't see you as a rival; they've been there and done it, anyway.

You must like them. As above, trust your intuition. Whoever wrote:

> *I do not love you, Dr Fell,*
> *But how or why, I cannot tell*

gave the doctor a wide berth if they had any sense. Don't allow anyone or anything to override your intuition. 'They're very respected...' 'Lots of other people speak highly of them...' So what?

Intuition doesn't get a lot of space in business literature, maybe because it's impossible to draw silly diagrams of it, complete with triangles, cutaway cylinders, more arrows than Custer's last stand and the word 'synergy' somewhere (you can tell I've suffered too many meetings run by people with MBAs). But intuition is hugely valuable, especially in dealing with people. Its lack of definability makes it hard to measure or to improve once you have made an assessment of it. This might appear bad news, but my experience of intuition is that almost everybody has it to a very high degree, and that the people who make bad judgements are the ones who override it in some way. If you make a run of bad judgements, ask yourself what you are putting in the way of your natural talent for spotting fakes and phonies.

Note that business has already ceased to be about spreadsheets and software, and has entered the world of personal judgement and emotions. Is this world 'easy'? As I said above, you have intuition. Trust it.

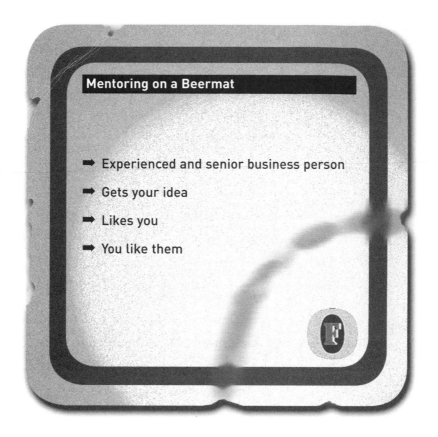

Mentoring on a Beermat

➡ Experienced and senior business person

➡ Gets your idea

➡ Likes you

➡ You like them

Business has already ceased to be about spreadsheets and software, and has entered the world of personal judgement and emotions.

What does a mentor offer?

At the most basic, a mentor offers *good advice*. They will have seen similar ideas before and will have an understanding about practical difficulties and (most important) how to get round these. They will have a broad view of the business marketplace and will understand where the idea fits in. They may know who is most likely to be receptive to your idea as a customer, not just which company but which person in that company.

They may even know that person and if so, this is where the mentor really earns your undying gratitude: *connections*. Anyone starting a business is depressingly familiar with interviews with well-meaning but powerless individuals from big organizations. Your enthusiastic presentation and their apparent fascination leads to 'I'll pass it on to Ms X' or 'I'll mention it at the next Z committee', after which nothing happens. Your mentor will send you direct to Ms X or to the chair of the Z committee *with a personal endorsement*. This should get you 15 minutes of that person's attention. Make sure you have a clear, concise, enthusiastic and appropriate 'pitch' ready for this. (I say 'appropriate' because you must have done your homework about *their* business before you meet them.)

Your mentor's connections are also essential if you need to raise *capital*. The mentor may invest themselves, or tell personal, and wealthy, friends. Or they can put you in touch with business angels or venture capitalists (VCs) – though read the section on funding before accepting large cheques from these people. Charlie Muirhead of Orchestream was finding it very hard to get even a response from Novell until Esther Dyson made a quick call to the chief technical officer.

Mentors are also invaluable in helping you find sources of *specialist advice*. (See the section on advisors on page 61.)

Why do people become mentors? Basically, because they enjoy it. Obviously it's not every successful business person's glass of Bollinger, and you will spot non-mentors very quickly, as they really do not want to be bothered by 'wannabes'. But to many people it is the ideal Indian summer of their career. As a mentor you can take part in a new business venture without having the total – and exhausting and risky – involvement of the team at the very core.

It's also rewarding at a deeper level. Mentors have a strong desire to pass on the lessons they have learned to the next generation, especially to people in whom they see at least a partial reflection of themselves.

It beats retirement, too. Many mentors get home from their last day at HQ with the cut glass and the retirement cheque, eager to get the roses sorted out and some fishing in. Two weeks later they are bored stiff.

There is also a financial inducement – the mentor should be rewarded with a paid, non-exec position in the organization. But this is not a major motive for a mentor, who should be well off enough anyway. If you suspect that money is their main motive, you have got the wrong person. Keep looking.

Finding a mentor is not easy, but it is worth every moment you put into the search many times over. Note that if you are lucky enough to find more than one mentor, choose the one you like best. The very close relationship between mentor and new business gets watered down by having more than one mentor. I have been in businesses where a whole advisory board of mentors has been in place – and has done nothing, as none of them felt any real ownership of the project.

Note that you now have a powerful endorsement, so your elevator pitch (Version 1.0) is complete. 'We make friction-free widgets. Sir Everard Polymath of Megacorp is on board.'

Your first customer

The third item on your Beermat Plan is your first customer. For the moment, enter the name in pencil. You can only use pen when they write you a cheque.

The journey to that point can be a long one, but it is a real adventure. You will have the satisfaction of seeing your idea mature as you undertake it. The truth is that, however good an idea is, it won't fit into the marketplace as neatly as you think. It's only by getting close to potential customers, by hearing precisely what they need, what they can afford and how they intend to purchase it, that you can really refine a business idea to the next hurdle – that first cheque.

This is your next big challenge after finding your mentor. Listening skills are essential here but also a measure of scepticism: comments not backed up by action are of limited value. Don't be knocked off

The truth is that, **however good** an idea is, it won't fit into the

marketplace

as neatly as you think.

course by well-meaning input from people who don't understand your idea or the market deeply enough. The sales cornerstone really comes into their own here, as they will naturally drive any potential customer to a 'close', i.e. a clear 'yes' with money attached, or a firm 'no' with clear reasons why.

Sending technical people into this kind of discussion can lead to fascinating debates about possible directions in widget design in the 22nd century but no clear commercial direction for your product, here, now. Leave the tech chat for conferences, and get the sales cornerstone earning their stake!

Remember that the ultimate judge of any commercial offering, from a corner shop to the whizziest internet application, is the *marketplace* – a truth which seemed to get forgotten during the dotcom bubble.

Seedling selling

Your mentor can often create golden sales leads for you via a word in the ear of someone senior at an ideal target company. Use and cherish these leads.

At the same time, think of other people who would benefit from your idea, and get selling to them. Remember that word benefit: you're selling *benefits to the customer*, not all those wonderful *features* that your technical team spent so long building into the product. I know you've read this before, probably in every book on selling you've ever seen, but people still seem to miss this point. Acres of rainforest still disappear every year just to provide pointless corporate puffery that has only one possible response: 'So what?'

When selling to other businesses – which is what you should be doing – the most attractive benefit is 'this will save you money'. Ideally this will be because your product does something new. Competition on pure price

– 'our widget is just like everyone else's, but cheaper' – is the worst kind of competition. Is it cheaper because it's poor quality? And for how long will you be the cheapest in the market? Quality of delivery, all the way from a cast-iron warranty to a smile on the face of the engineer, becomes a competitive factor once you are up and running and once customers can judge the delivery for themselves. (But start off on the right foot anyway; be nice to deal with from day one.) 'Lifestyle' competition, on which many consumer markets thrive, is by far the hardest to make work. 'Our widgets are cooler!' 'Says who?'

Here is a 'hierarchy of benefits'.

1 Saves money by solving problem in a new way.

2 Saves money by solving problem in an old way, but more cheaply.

3 Quality of service – 'hard stuff', warranties, etc.

4 Quality of service – 'soft stuff'. Nice to deal with.

5 'Lifestyle'.

6 Pure price ('we're crap, but at least we don't cost you much').

Rule one of selling is to understand your customers' needs. Rule two is to know your product and its benefits inside out. You begin to sell once you match your customers' needs with your product's benefits.

Time to go and pitch

Selling is always person to person. Brochures, videos and so on are never a substitute for human contact. This is why your mentor's endorsement, and their phone call to the boss of a potential client, is so valuable. But if this is not available, how do you find the right person to speak to?

It's a bit like finding your mentor. Get e-mailing and calling. If you are unendorsed, you won't speak to the MD straight off, but *someone* will answer the phone or reply to the e-mail. Get into a dialogue with them about your product and its benefits, and ask for their help. 'Who should I be speaking to?' 'What's the best way to contact them?' Phone answerers can be extraordinarily helpful.

When you get to talk to the person you should be talking to, introduce yourself, use your elevator pitch and ask for a brief meeting. Fifteen minutes, that's all you want.

When you secure this *initial* meeting, your pitch will be longer, of course, but still keep it simple. Three big benefits maximum; one big benefit will do. The content should vary from audience to audience: it is a description of how your product will benefit *them,* not why your product is wonderful in the general scheme of things.

When making your pitch, don't feel that the longer you talk to people the more interested they are. This isn't true. Customers often 'go off the boil' in meetings and sit listening to people they've decided not to buy from, out of a mixture of politeness, laziness (it's easier than working) and an ever-diminishing hope that you might suddenly say something that actually does interest them.

You should go into every meeting you ever have with a clear objective. Here, an order is the ideal, but more likely it will be something else useful such as an agreement to a trial or a further meeting – a sign that you've passed their initial 'sanity check'.

At the *next* meeting, you are definitely after an order. If you've got this far, the customer should have a real need for what you have to offer. Watch out for team meetings where everyone is keen to talk theory and technicalities and not about specifically how your product is going to be of use to them: you may be being pumped for information. But most such meetings, if set up properly and *led by your sales cornerstone*, should lead to a real outcome, either a yes or a no with unambiguous reasons.

Much seedling selling is like consultancy. Consultancy can be a dirty word in business circles, conjuring up preppy MBAs telling people twice their age things they know already and charging them a fortune. But the good consultant listens very carefully to what they are told, interprets that in the light of their knowledge and delivers a judgement that has real value.

You should be doing the same. You don't have a proven product to sell, but by listening carefully and thinking deeply about the client's real needs and how your offer can meet those needs, you can make a sale.

Ideally, you sell to the client so well that they agree to pay at least part of the price in advance. This is an outcome really worth striving for (see the section below on finance).

Whenever your first customer writes out your first cheque, it's a very special moment indeed. Savour it. Once the cheque has cleared, retrieve it, frame it and hang it on your wall.

You've fulfilled your Beermat Plan.

The team

The ideal team for a seedling enterprise is the entrepreneur, four cornerstones and the mentor. The mentor isn't a part of the day-to-day team, however: on this, most basic, level, the business is run by a team of *five individuals*.

Five is a magic number. Look at the great names of rock'n'roll. Boyzone, Westlife, Steps. Those wild men of rock'n'roll, Five themselves. Seriously: Oasis, The Rolling Stones, The Beatles if you include the essential contributions of Brian Epstein and then Sir George Martin.

'Five is a **magic** number'

This isn't just hearsay – oops, there's another example – there is, I believe, a reason for this. Two people are a marriage. Three people are a marriage plus an outsider. Four people are two marriages. This may sound silly, but groups of four so often split into two feuding individuals watched by two passive ones (look at The Beatles once they had cut themselves adrift from Sir George). Five just seems to be the number that works. It's big enough for flexibility, for grouping and regrouping of individuals round different ideas at different times. It's too small for cliques to form within it. And it's odd, so a majority vote can always be taken.

The cornerstones do not have to be full-time from Day One. None of them does, though the entrepreneur will really only be happy when working on the idea. I advise keeping some form of other income, even if it's only part-time, for as long as possible, though I sympathize with anyone who jacks in a job to really get stuck into the fulfilment of their entrepreneurial dream. Like lovers who elope, it's not hugely sensible, but that's not really the point.

What should the five-person team look like? My ideal line-up is as follows.

➡ The *entrepreneur*. The person with the vision and the charisma. The boss.

➡ The *technical innovator*. The brains behind the product. 'Supernerd.'

➡ The *delivery* specialist. Also a technician, but in the very different area of delivery. In America, these people often become chief operating officer (COO), but this is not a title I find useful (anyway, this is the UK edition).

➡ The *sales* specialist. No revenue, no business!

➡ The *financier*. Keeps costs under strict control.

Note: the entrepreneur will probably come from a sales or technical background. They still need all four cornerstones in their start-up team, however. This is very important.

The entrepreneur's job is to keep the flame of the business's vision ablaze, both internally and when presenting the company to outsiders: to the media and to potential customers. They will probably still initiate some sales or do bits of technical work, but they must pass the core responsibility for the area where they once reigned supreme over to the more reliable cornerstones. This isn't easy, but it must be done.

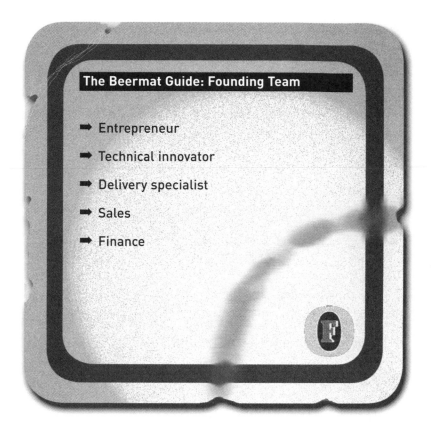

The Beermat Guide: Founding Team

➡ Entrepreneur

➡ Technical innovator

➡ Delivery specialist

➡ Sales

➡ Finance

There's another helpful little acronym. All you need is ETDSF!

Now comes the really radical bit. I'm convinced that these five people should be *equal* shareholders in the company.

I'll say that again.
Equal shareholders.

Many entrepreneurs get very defensive when this five-way split is suggested. 'I thought of the idea!' But business is a team game and if your team is anything less than passionate, you won't win. A 20 per cent stake gets the right people and gives them the right motivation, which isn't just financial but is about belonging.

Entrepreneurs also fear they will lose control if this five-way split is instituted. While that is technically true, a structure will soon emerge for day-to-day running of the business, with the entrepreneur at the top and the four cornerstones reporting to them. The entrepreneur is still effectively the boss, and every company must have a boss, there is no way around this. But with equal shareholdings for all, the boss has to listen very hard to the clever and passionate specialists around them, and this is exactly how it should be.

When the company gets bigger, the entrepreneur and the cornerstones (plus non-execs) will be the board. This board *must* be strong, and the only way to build strength into it is to empower its members. I have seen so many companies where one individual, usually the entrepreneur, owns up to 80 per cent of the stock. And I've seen so many of them fail: the owner gets a crazy new idea or simply refuses to listen to warnings. Majority owners always have a gun to point at their team members: in the last resort, they can sack everybody or sell the business. And entrepreneurs aren't the most level-headed of people.

The board must be strong and the only way to build strength into it is to empower its members.

If you are an entrepreneur and are still not convinced, consider that 80 per cent of a business that has failed because the one person in charge became arrogant and screwed it up is worth nothing, while 20 per cent of a company that has been properly nurtured and now has a value of £10 million is – well, 'do the math'.

On a less radical note, observe that there are *two* technical corner-stones. This applies to any business I can think of. In a software business, the innovators are writing early versions of the software, up to 1.0. The delivery specialist then takes over, improving piecemeal – Versions 1.1, 1.2, 1.3, etc. – while the innovator starts pulling the whole thing to bits and reassembling it to create Version 2.0. In a manufac-turing business, the innovator's skill is about design, function, construction, materials application; the delivery specialist concentrates on processes, machinery, manning, cost efficiency, materials handling.

Which cornerstone should be in charge of basic admin? It can be the 'delivery specialist', but I think the best person for the job is the finance cornerstone. They will have a natural feel for value for money. The worst person is definitely the entrepreneur – if you let them loose in this area, it is only a matter of time before you come into the office one morning to find gold taps in the washroom, specially imported papyrus notepaper and amazing new telephones with video screens that don't quite work at the moment but the bloke who invented them is coming in next week to fix them. And no milk in the fridge.

The Instruction Set, the business I co-founded, started with a visionary entrepreneur, an innovator and me, a salesman. We all started full-time straight away, found ourselves another techie, then a finance corner-stone who was at the time a vice president (VP) at Goldman Sachs. (Yes, he did join us full-time later.) The ground-plan for the five-person team was laid out (as above) very early on, then the right people were found to fill those positions.

Wanted: four cornerstones

How do you find these 'right people'? There should be a nucleus of you; two or three, to start off with. The entrepreneur's magnetism will have attracted a group of individuals with, hopefully, a range of business skills.

Supposing this isn't the case? Supposing you're an entrepreneur plus a techie only? Conventional wisdom says 'hire in accountants or sales people'. But you hardly ever get the right kind of people – proper cornerstones, with their unique mixture of solidity and entrepreneurial flair – that way.

A group of techies without an entrepreneur is in an even worse position. You will not get your business off the ground. If a group of you have a good idea but lack the fire and charisma (and selfishness!) of the entrepreneur, find such a person *you can trust*. Someone with a sales background would be ideal: sales people need great ideas to sell like fish need water. (Note: don't be fooled by stereotypes of men in loud ties on used car lots. Proper sales people are not loud and aggressive but likeable, confident and good listeners.)

The best place to look for cornerstones is among the people you know. The Instruction Set formed this way. The techies had co-authored a book on Unix; I was in a brilliantly witty student revue (I should know, I wrote it) for which one of the techies ran the sound and lights; the other techie had the entrepreneur on the MSc course he was teaching. The financier? Why, the entrepreneur's brother, of course.

Your mentor may also have suggestions, but look among your personal contacts first.

Because I have been in business a long time, I now have a list of people I know personally and whom I know would make good cornerstones. I use this list whenever I am involved in a start-up. If you do not have such a list, think about developing one. Remember that it's not a list of ideal people from 'out there' but people you know and like.

Supposing you have exhausted your contacts, and your mentor's contacts, and still have gaps? One simple answer is 'wait'. The entrepreneur will be networking anyway, and they will meet the right person in time. Right now is a particularly good time to be looking for cornerstones, as there are plenty of people who cut their entrepreneurial teeth on dot-coms that have gone bust. If they are any good, they will have learned a lot from that experience and be ready to have another go – using a more grown-up growth model this time.

If possible, offer them the market rate for what they do (can be expensive for accountants!), but a real cornerstone will be in this for adequate money, lots of fun and huge long-term potential. If the potential cornerstone starts getting niggly about money, they are not right for the job. Maybe they haven't quite got over dot-com mania, where some people were paid ludicrous salaries. My recommendation for such deluded souls is that they spend six months as a hospital porter or staff nurse, after which they might have recovered from the idea that the world automatically owes them £250,000 p.a.

Don't ever take on someone because they 'look good on paper'. I wouldn't take on an assistant toilet cleaner on this kind of 'recommendation', and here we're talking about someone who will effectively be a blood brother or sister for the next five years of your life.

Being sure

Once you have a good candidate, how do you *know* that an individual is right for the team? There are supposed to be profiling systems that fit people for roles, but these are appallingly blunt instruments. I've never seen any useful result from these systems: they either tell you what you know already or come up with half-baked recommendations, like those astrologers who tell you that you will have quite a good day today though there might be a few bad bits in it.

Cornerstones are people you like and who like you.

You possess a much subtler instrument anyway: your intuition.

Like your mentor, cornerstones are people you like and who like you. They are also people you trust, both as to their professional skill and to their personal integrity. And they genuinely believe both in the idea and in the entrepreneur's ability to steer it through to success.

The process of choosing cornerstones is like choosing friends, which is why personal recommendation is the best place to start. Note however that if they *are* friends, your friendship will suffer: once you become founder members of a seedling business, you are working for a higher cause and your interactions will become subordinate to that cause. You may find yourself arguing bitterly. Only if you sell the business will the friendship sprout up again.

Remember, the aim is to find and then forge a group of five equals who will run the company for the rest of its life, or at least well into its 'mighty oak' stage. Take your time if you must. Get it right.

When you have your four cornerstones in place – the right four people, with the right skills, commitment and passion for the enterprise – your idea has leapt another hurdle, that of totally convincing four very able people to commit themselves to it.

33

The long haul

Cornerstones aren't short-termers. They're in this for the long haul. And they're prepared to give it all they've got.

Such commitment can be stressful. Make sure you set rules about things like holidays. At The Instruction Set we came to the conclusion that everyone should be made to take two full, consecutive weeks' holiday every year. During this time nobody at work was allowed to contact them. If we could kidnap their mobile phone, we did.

Long commutes also cause stress. If you're going to be living and breathing a business for five years, move close to it. Walking or cycling distance, preferably.

All this points to the desirability of becoming an entrepreneur before you acquire a family. Of course, if you have a family, this does not disqualify you from enterprise (any more than age does: Ray Kroc founded McDonald's in his fifties). But if you are in your early twenties, unattached and eager to found a business, bear this in mind.

Non-execs

As well as cornerstones, you can have other sources of leadership at your disposal. Your mentor should be a non-executive chairman or director of the business. And how about some other non-executive directors? These are people who don't have the intimate connection to the business that the founding five have, but who bring to it expert knowledge, and do so with the mentor's motivation of interest and involvement rather than hard cash.

As with cornerstones, recruit non-execs personally. They are part of the team, remember. When you've done so, use them well. They have expertise and influence, but can use these only if you are totally honest

Go and ask their help and it's amazing what they can do.

with them. It's no use treating them like a teacher or parent you want to hide things from (don't laugh, I've seen people do it). The more they know, warts and all, the more help they can be.

Non-execs can be of particular use if you have one specific problem that none of you five founders seem able to solve. Go and ask their help, and it's amazing what they can do.

Sadly, however, not all non-execs fall into the above category. There are two types of non-exec who are worse than useless.

One is the 'letterhead non-exec'. I have seen several companies where retired celebs or members of the aristocracy are made non-exec directors, in a bid to impress people with their name on the notepaper. This is silly: nobody of any importance is impressed by this. Of course, if the celeb/aristo has contacts that they really can activate, then they can earn their fee.

The other is the externally appointed non-exec. These people are placed on boards by external equity holders, usually venture capitalists (VCs). My experience of such people is that they a) have no experience of running businesses and b) spend board meetings quibbling about minutiae, raising irrelevant points and generally trying to show everyone how clever they are (and achieving the opposite effect). Of course, if you've given a chunk of your business to a VC, you may well have to put up with this kind of idiot. So try to find other sources of finance. The topic of VCs gets a healthy airing later on in this book!

So, choose non-execs whom you respect, who have contacts and experience, who bring a fresh perspective to the party, and who are nice people to work with.

How to compete

Now you are truly in business, I should say a bit about how to compete. I'm a great believer in competition – it drives innovation and stops businesses becoming smug and arrogant towards their customers. But it isn't a religion. There comes a point where competitiveness becomes destructive, both to the business and to the individuals practising it.

When you start selling your product, you will inevitably hear people say, 'So it's a bit like the widgets that ABC make.' Imagine these two responses...

Salesperson A:

'Them! We hate those guys. Their stuff is rubbish .'

Salesperson B:

'Oh, yes, ABC. I've heard they're a good company and make a good product. But our product offers these special benefits...'

It sounds obvious which is the more mature approach, but I have heard – and been horrified by – grown, adult, highly paid sales people reacting like A.

When I run a sales department, bad-mouthing the opposition is a disciplinable, and ultimately sackable, offence. Customers may well know people in the opposition and will probably have been using their products quite happily for years. Are you telling them they're stupid? Anyway, customers are not interested in squabbles between suppliers; they are interested in getting their needs met. If you can do better than the opposition, prove it in a positive way.

'Slagging off the oppo' competition often has bad personal side effects, too. People who practise it seem to become less pleasant, and less happy. One of the purposes of this book is to help readers make money but not lose their souls: becoming twisted with loathing for United Widgets PLC is not the way to a full, rich life.

When I run sales teams, I keep competition at a level where you can have a drink with the opposition and conduct a proper conversation with them. Sport played in the right spirit has the same credo. Hard, fair competition on the field; a drink in the bar afterwards.

Supposing the opposition get rough? Sport provides a good analogy again. Gary Lineker was on the receiving end of numerous fouls, but he never let them put him off his job, which was to score goals. One of the purposes of dirty tactics is to take the victim's mind off their proper task, which in business is serving the customer.

The white paper

You've sold your idea. Then you deliver it and the customer is satisfied. Better, the customer is delighted. It did what you said it would, apart from a few glitches which you went in and fixed straight away, at no extra cost.

The idea has just leapt over its seventh hurdle. It has become a proper product, and it's time to set out the nature and benefits of that product, formally. You do this in a white paper. This is a semi-technical document, explaining the product and its real value proposition in depth, including as much about how it is being used by your first customer as confidentiality will allow. It should be no longer than 10 sides (some people let it run to 20, but I prefer brevity). Page one should be an executive summary of the following nine, stressing the three (or fewer) main benefits the product has brought. If you can get your customer to write your white paper, even better.

Before sending it to potential *new* customers, have your mentor read through it. They will view it from a customer's eye-view. I wrote the white paper for RiverSoft and gave it to Sir Campbell, who returned it much shortened, as it was too full of technical stuff (i.e. *features*), which overshadowed the sections on actual commercial *benefits*.

The white paper has two purposes. Externally, it is to send to prospects before a first meeting, to familiarize them with your product so that at that meeting they ask the right questions, about how the product can really help them. Internally, it concentrates the team on where the product has got to, which may now be something very different from your good-enough idea in the pub.

The idea has just leapt over its seventh hurdle. It has become a proper product.

Beyond the first sale

Your first sale was a great moment: you were right to celebrate it. But don't get carried away and start ramping up borrowing and spending. You must now start building a portfolio of customers. The aim should be to have 10 or 15 regular customers, none of whom is responsible for more than 15 per cent of your income, plus a back-up list of 20 potential customers whom you are researching and getting to know. As this begins to come about, your business starts to change. You need to start taking people on. Planning becomes more complicated and more important.

You are growing into a sapling enterprise.

Sometimes, sadly, you make one sale, get your white paper all written up, then all goes quiet. Despite all your best efforts, you've made one sale and no more. It's unusual, but it can happen.

You need to ask yourself what the market really is for your product. Maybe there is only one buyer. If so, you must diversify. What else can you do with the skills that developed that product so successfully? (It *is* a success, as someone has bought it.) Can you sell more things to your one, satisfied customer? (Not an ideal situation, as suppliers to Marks and Spencer have found out, but better than no business at all.) If neither of these options seems to work, it might be necessary to pull the plug. Don't give up easily, but if you really have tried all possible avenues and still made only a single, one-off sale, don't be ashamed to get working on something new.

However, by far the most likely outcome is that further sales will follow. Start thinking in terms of that portfolio of actual and potential customers.

Early pricing

Pricing something new is hard. Just how much is it worth? It's always wise to look round the market at products most like yours. Be humble: few products are actually as radical as the originators believe them to be. What is your nearest rival and what do they charge?

But that's only a guideline. What *really* matters in pricing is how much the product is worth to the customer, which is closely related to how much money it will make (or, more likely, save) them. So the more you know about your customer's business – not just roughly what they make and do, but the precise details of how they do it and at what cost – the better placed you are to guess the right price for your product. Your sales cornerstone should be talking to your main potential customers in depth anyway: listen to them.

Don't be in a hurry to issue a formal price list. You are not yet delivering standard products. Delivery will still involve a lot of customization, and even outright invention, this early in a business.

If you are fully funded, you can offer early adopters low prices, on the clear understanding that the prices will rise as they use your product more and more. Don't try to fool people into buying cheap, then turn round and sting them with a price hike: let them know in advance

Be humble:
few products are actually
as radical
as the originators believe them to be.

of your pricing plans. If they like your product and it clearly makes or saves them money, they will be happy to pay a fair rate.

Remember that while nobody likes to pay more for something than they have to, the ultimate aim of all negotiation is 'win-win' situations, where each party gains.

The real business plan

I have very little time for business plans for products that have not yet made any sales. It's not that the underlying ideas are rubbish, but they are untested and unrefined. As such, nobody really knows whether they will sell or not. All this talk of capturing a 5 per cent share of a £200 million market in five years is moonshine, if nobody's actually bought a single example of the product yet. Future generations will roar with laughter at the very idea of this, but the dot-com bubble was pumped up on exactly these kinds of absurd extrapolations of sales figures from zero into a rosy future.

But once you have started making sales, you do need a business plan. A *real* business plan. You have a real idea of what your market is and who your rivals are going to be. You have one actual and several potential customers, and should have some idea of how much they are likely to buy and when. You need to plan your recruitment strategy, your cash flow...

Like the white paper, the real business plan has internal and external value. Internally (its biggest benefit), it focuses the team. Externally, it will be of use if you find yourself in need of development capital (but see the section on funding below: people get real benefit from what you produce, so try to get them to pay up front for it!).

The contents of the real business plan are outlined overleaf.

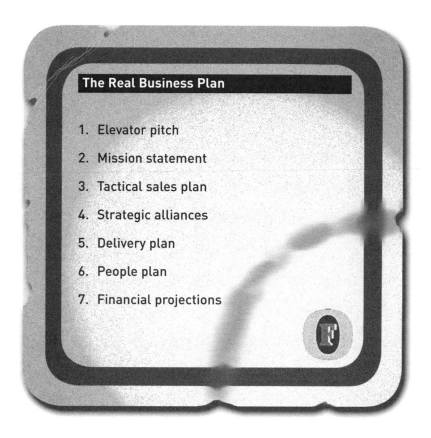

The Real Business Plan

1. Elevator pitch

2. Mission statement

3. Tactical sales plan

4. Strategic alliances

5. Delivery plan

6. People plan

7. Financial projections

The tactical sales plan (3) lists your next ten customers, and what you intend to sell them in what time frame. The delivery plan (5) outlines how they will be delivered, and section (4) covers any strategic alliances you intend to form to make these sales happen. The people plan (6) is probably the most important section, and the one accountants look at least. Who is going to do what? Will you need to hire new people, and if so, what sort of people and when? How will everybody's performance be measured?

When you draw up this plan, don't be afraid to get help. MBA students are ideal for this sort of thing. Find one who isn't appallingly arrogant – they do exist, I promise – and get them to help you draw up the plan. Employ a market specialist to make market assessments sound (and be) convincing. You should have a financial cornerstone in place by now, but if you haven't, get a bright business school student to help you draw up the spreadsheets.

Note that if the MBA or the student click with you and the team, they may come and join you. In the sapling stage, bright, young team members are what you need.

Mission statement

It's easy to be cynical about mission statements, but they are of great value. Missions are about purpose. What is the purpose of this company? Not just 'to make money', that's not enough nowadays. Who are our customers? What benefits are we going to provide for them? What are we going to do to ensure that they keep on sourcing these benefits from us? What is our company going to look like to the world out there? What will it be like to work in?

I think the last question is hugely important, and the answer should be 'fun'. The dour old Dickensian image of work is history. The best people are motivated by enthusiasm, passion, purpose – by a mission.

The dour old Dickensian image of work is **history.** The best people are motivated by **enthusiasm, passion, purpose –** by a mission.

Strategic alliances

This might seem a rather pompous term to have in so youthful a document as your real business plan (the company is still only one sale old!), but it is never too early to start thinking about strategic alliances. Who could you help sell more of their product? No matter how big they are, if you think you can help, then talk to them. Get them to trial one of their machines featuring your widget, or to have a section in their shop selling your ethically made clothes.

Though the sales cornerstone may have views on this, it is the entrepreneur who is most likely to suggest alliances. It is certainly part of the entrepreneur's job to set up such alliances, partially because of that perpetually useful charisma; partially because as chief executive officer (CEO) they can approach senior people in big companies on a 'level footing'; partially because, when all's said and done, they remain the overall expert on the business, its markets and direction.

For a small company that believes it can be a real strategic partner to a big one, an excellent place to approach the big fish is at trade shows, where top sales people from the big one are often manning stands and keen to talk to people. Take them off for a drink, get them talking about their customers' needs and how, maybe, you could help. They may not 'bite', in which case you at least tried, but if your product is good and you have done your homework, you stand a good chance of success.

In the software/hi-tech industry, the best strategic partners are manufacturers, not service companies. The logo of a big service provider might look good on your website, but they can drop alliances very quickly.

The real business plan is effectively a blueprint for the transition to the next stage in the company's life. Once you start making those planned next 10 sales, you will need to start taking on people to deliver against them, and the glory days of the five of you against the world will be over. Shame, in a way – business may never be quite as much fun. But you have no option but to move on, so do so joyfully. Onward and upward!

Before moving to the next stage, however, there are plenty of issues still to be discussed about life in the seedling stage. Most important of all is probably...

Finance

The finance cornerstone has two main issues to deal with. One is the overall funding of the business, the other is the day-to-day control of its costs. They need to be expert at both.

In this section I shall set out some tips from our finance manager at The Instruction Set, Rick Medlock, then make some observations about funding.

➡ Always get the finance cornerstone and the entrepreneur to sign the cheques, at least until you have grown significantly, so that a) there is good control and b) you actually see what your hard-earned cash is being spent on.

➡ Always borrow on a long-term basis if you can; an overdraft can be called in at any time whereas a lease or a three-year term loan gives you certainty of cash flow.

➡ Always do a cash flow forecast and always take a gloomier picture than your worst estimates.

➡ Try to persuade suppliers to give you extra payment terms – 60 rather than 30 days to pay.

➡ Don't mess with the VAT man, Inland Revenue or DSS. If you get on the wrong side of them, they will be after you for ever and will scrutinize everything you do or claim.

➡ Get your systems and documentation process right from day one. Too many people simply start, then worry about the audit trail or evidence for expenses afterwards. This inevitably leads to problems. Set up simple manual systems – files of invoices, all expenses requiring receipts, time reporting – on day one. There are simple accounting systems for PCs (such as Mind Your Own Business) which are available very cheaply. They will need to be replaced when you are ready to become as big as Logica, but on day one they are ideal and cheap.

➡ Don't spend money that you don't have in the vain hope that money will be found somewhere. *This is the quickest route to bankruptcy.* If you haven't actually got the cash today, don't spend it. If you want to commit to some big expense, such as a new employee on a high salary, make sure that you know where the cash is coming from to pay them.

➡ Treat capital expenditure even more suspiciously than day-to-day expenses. Ignore the fact that these assets last for more than one year (and therefore you think they are worth something to someone else). The truth is that used computers are basically worth zip to anyone else. Just remember that the cash goes out of the door on day one! Try to lease them by all means, but remember you have to keep paying that lease for as long as the lease lasts.

➡ Try to get the credit rating people like Dun & Bradstreet on side. Your credit rating determines whether suppliers will give you credit or demand cash, so always make time to talk to these people, to see them and send them up-to-date, well-presented information.

➡ Whether you are borrowing or not, keep the bank well informed and up to date on progress, and again give them good information so that if you want to borrow to expand, they know you and your business and they trust you.

This is the quickest route to bankruptcy. If you haven'tactually got the cash today, don't spend it.

Sir Campbell Fraser's advice to finance cornerstones is even more succinct. 'Watch the cash, laddie.'

Seedling funding

At The Instruction Set, we built a 150-person company without any substantial outside funding. I recommend you do the same, partly because external funding is a nightmare, but mainly because refusing to rely on it imposes a financial and sales discipline on the business that is very, very healthy.

This is a return to the 'organic model': funding growth out of revenue. This is not just a reaction to the absurdity of the dot-com bubble; it's what I believe to be the best foundation for a successful business.

There are, of course, exceptions. A biotech company will hardly be able to develop a world-beating drug on early revenue plus a few hundred thousand from a friend of the mentor. But it would be better off partnering with a well-chosen big pharma company than selling its soul to the City, as investors in companies like British Biotech found out in the 1990s. If at all possible, avoid outside funding, and if you must fund externally, get more than money, get a real, value-adding partner in the business.

Here is my list of funding sources, in descending order of desirability:

First and best is your own money. If you've got it. Most of us don't have this kind of money, but if you do, use it, but only money you can afford to lose.

Family money is different. There are success stories about business founded with family money – Easyjet is a recent example – but an awful lot of 'family money' ventures seem to fail. There may be obscure Freudian reasons behind this, but I think it is more likely just 'easy come, easy go'. Unless you have had to sweat for the money, you'll bottle out of those tough financial decisions at the margin that can make the difference between success and failure.

Money borrowed from friends seems to suffer the same fate of vanishing too easily. The friendship usually vanishes with it.

Second, for those of us who don't have private money, there may be grants or loans available from institutions such as The Prince's Trust. The trust is an excellent organization, which really does want to help young people with bright ideas. The government also runs a range of schemes: contact your local Business Link (the address will be in the phone book) for details. But beware the long lead times that can be involved in securing funding from these sources, and remember that the entrepreneur will have a much shorter attention span than the financial cornerstone.

Third, revenue. If you have a product that sounds capable of making a real difference to your customers' business, ask for payment in advance. Your customer may need reassurance on quality and delivery. Provide it. You want to be the best anyway. They may ask for a discount for advance payment. As long as this isn't *a lot* more expensive than a bank loan, accept it.

Your customer may **need** reassurance on quality and delivery. Provide it.

We secured a healthy chunk of early finance this way at The Instruction Set, selling our first Advanced Unix course to a client in Sweden. We hadn't actually written the course at the time, and soon after receiving the advance payment, one of our main 'gurus' fell ill. We had to get the course ready, by hook or by crook. And, of course, we did. I remember the day before the course was due to begin, sitting in our office punching holes in pages and putting them into loose-leaf binders. The plane was due to leave in two hours. But of course that's exactly the fun of starting a business.

Fourth, your mentor. If your mentor really likes you and your idea, they may well make an investment themselves. They are part of the team, and this investment cements the relationship. Note that the mentor's true motive is fun, not profit. But at the same time, it is not 'soft money', like daddy's or a friend's.

Fifth, a friend of the mentor, who is also investing for the pleasure of involvement rather than straight financial gain.

After these, there comes a big, big gap. Are you really sure none of the above avenues are open to you? Think again, as next comes…

Sixth, bank lending.

I have a problem with banks. If they lend you a tiny fraction of what your business could make if it takes off, they demand personal guarantees that give them the power to chuck you and your family out onto the street. I think this is appalling. If the government were serious about promoting an enterprise culture, it would make this illegal. Few people start a business frivolously, and banks ought to be able to spot these. The failure of a business venture is a heartbreaking and exhausting experience for the overwhelming majority of entrepreneurs. For the banks to punish them further is monstrous. Don't believe those cuddly ads on TV: there is still the soul of a vicious Dickensian miser, no doubt with a suitably Dickensian name like Grippile or Cringebottom, at the heart of every bank's lending-to-small-business operation.

Banks will no doubt moan that since they are not taking a stake in your company, there is no 'upside' to their lending policy, so they must protect themselves. I disagree – there is a considerable upside, namely your continued custom if your business prospers.

After the banks, things get even worse, as you have to start handing out chunks of equity.

Seventh in my list of finance sources is a 'strategic option', where a customer agrees to pay in advance but insists on the right to invest money in the company at a preferential rate when you next raise finance. This is the nicest form of losing equity. You get some money up front, and when the options are exercised you lose a chunk of equity, but you have a partner on board who lives and breathes your business, rather than a financial institution that just looks at the money that comes out of the end of it. But you've still lost a chunk of your company. There is also a freedom issue. Think this through carefully before entering such an agreement. Will your new partner start calling the shots? Will you be able to do business with their rivals?

Despite these objections, this 'strategic stake' became a popular form of investment in the late 1990s, and though the options craze of that era died with dotcom mania, it is still a popular solution to funding problems.

Eighth on my list come business angels, individuals with typically up to £1 million to invest in enterprises that attract them. I actually like these people. They love business; they can provide mentorship; they really get involved in the project. But they can be greedy: they usually demand a big stake. The locus of power in your organization should remain inside the founding team. Never offer more than 25 per cent. If the idea flies, the angel will still make an enormous profit.

Your mentor should be able to suggest angels. If not, there are formal networks of angels, such as Venture Capital Report. Go to Venturefest, an annual fair held in Oxford where angels and entrepreneurs get together, or if you're in Scotland, contact Connect.

Ninth, venture capital houses. These tend to deal in much bigger sums. Details of the minimum loan sizes of the different VC houses are available on the website of the British Venture Capital Association (www.bvca.co.uk), but most of them won't look at deals under £2 million. It is often the case that angels fund the start-up of a business, then VCs come in later, when the product is proven but needs development.

But don't be dazzled by this glittering pile of money. VC investment reminds me of the story of Dr Faustus, who sold his soul to the devil. Initially Faustus had everything he wanted and more, but in the end Old Nick came and took away the doctor's soul. The ultimate asset-strip.

VC houses will try to throw more money at you than you actually need in return for a bigger stake in your business than it is healthy for them to have. They also have a nasty habit of ratcheting up that stake if things start going a little wrong, and can flog you off to the highest bidder whenever they feel like it – 'rolling over' (i.e. indefinitely postponing) all those nice payouts they promised you in the process.

Unlike angels, VCs are in it purely for the money and are very focused on the short term. They're the kind of people Will Hutton is always complaining about. Whatever they tell you, their horizon is three years, max, and they will not be tolerant of hold-ups and glitches. Note that, as an odd part of this 'short-termism', they suffer from an addiction to fads only otherwise found in teenagers. In the past 18 months, VCs have known for a fact that the future of business will lie in b2c, then in b2b, then in infrastructure plays and, at the time of writing, in 'intellectual property and experienced teams'. They're a kind of refined version of the talent-spotting people in music companies, always eager to sign up bands who sound like today's number one.

Anything to be said in favour of VCs? They do have access to serious amounts of money, so if you really need that money *and can find no other way to get it*, then apply to them.

Talk to your mentor about the different VC houses and how they operate. Talk to anyone and everyone else about this, too. Somewhere

VC investment
reminds me of the story of
Dr Faustus,
who sold his soul
to the devil.

out there, there may be a VC who is a genuine investor, a person who wants to share your passion and who has access to all sorts of outside help in areas where entrepreneurs are usually weak. This ideal VC will find you a brilliant marketing and human resources (HR) director when the time comes for employing such people. They will attend board meetings and give intelligent advice based on the broad knowledge of business they have gained from their portfolio of investments. They will find customers for you and give you endorsements.

The trouble is, of all the many VCs I've met, only one has been like this.

A friend who runs a marketing consultancy for VCs assures me that since the dot-com disaster, VCs are cleaning up their act and really working on adding value to their investments rather than playing casinos with them. I'm yet to be convinced.

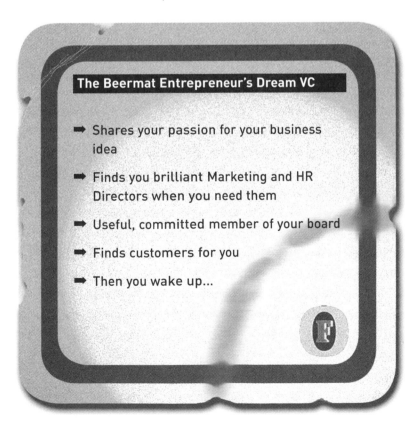

The Beermat Entrepreneur's Dream VC

➡ Shares your passion for your business idea

➡ Finds you brilliant Marketing and HR Directors when you need them

➡ Useful, committed member of your board

➡ Finds customers for you

➡ Then you wake up...

The moment you have VCs in your business, you will know why it was so crucial to have **five strong people** running the seedling.

Still, if you really must pitch to VCs, build your pitch round the finance cornerstone. Have the entrepreneur talk about the vision for five minutes before getting the sales cornerstone to talk about real customers. Then hand over to the financier, who can talk spreadsheets and cash flow – the language that VCs, who are largely accountants, understand. Finally, get your mentor to close the pitch with an endorsement. Don't let anyone technical within several miles of the pitch.

The moment you have VCs in your business, you will know why it was so crucial to have five strong people running the seedling, rather than the entrepreneur plus various tame sidekicks. Even in the best circumstances, there will be battles between the new part-owners and the original team, and if you want to keep your vision alive, you five will all have to fight for it.

You've probably gathered I'm not a huge fan of VCs. I blame them in part for the dot-com bubble. I think they are far too interested in money and far too little interested in what business is really about: people, change and customers. I accept that in some cases they have helped businesses grow, but most of the entrepreneurs I know hate them. Sorry, but that's how it is.

Are there any other sources of cash? There's always organized crime, I suppose, but the debt collection methods are a bit radical.

So my advice on funding is *stay organic*. Move heaven and earth to avoid outside financial involvement in your business. If you must have outsiders, do not be blinded by money: find backers who really bring something to the party in terms of enthusiasm, expertise or solid-gold contacts.

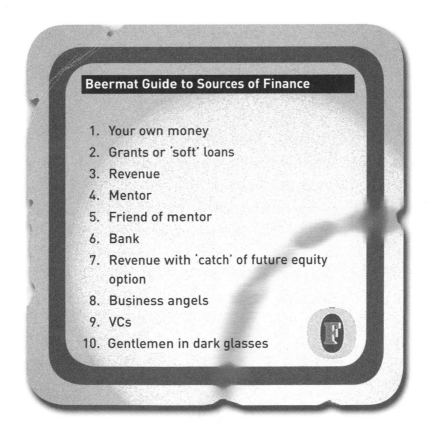

Beermat Guide to Sources of Finance

1. Your own money
2. Grants or 'soft' loans
3. Revenue
4. Mentor
5. Friend of mentor
6. Bank
7. Revenue with 'catch' of future equity option
8. Business angels
9. VCs
10. Gentlemen in dark glasses

The law

You don't need an in-house lawyer. Legal advice is best bought in for *essential legal work* such as partnership agreements, leases, warranties and employment contracts. The best lawyers have standard formulae for these: boilerplate contracts with schedules to particularize them. These should cost hundreds rather than thousands of pounds. Bad lawyers string out work; don't let them get away with it.

Lawyers who do string out work sometimes complain that they have been given such a poor brief that it's taken them all this time to understand what their clients really want. Maybe that's true sometimes. Certainly don't leave yourself open to this response. Be clear with these guys.

As usual, ask your mentor for advice when selecting your lawyers. When you have made your choice, get the finance cornerstone to deal with them. Financial minds are much closer to legal ones than technical, sales or entrepreneurial minds are, and the finance cornerstone will keep an eye on legal costs.

Registration

For legal and tax reasons, you should consider becoming a private limited company (technically, a 'private company limited by shares') from day one – certainly from that second meeting in the pub when you draw up the Beermat Plan. Your business will then be called 'Wizziwidgets *Limited*' and can have 50 shareholders. You can remain a private limited company for ever, and I recommend such a course of action (see the comments about stock exchange listing later on). You can do this registration yourself, but it takes time better spent elsewhere. Any good law firm will have a fixed-price service whereby they will register a company 'off the shelf' for you.

Off-the-shelf companies come complete with odd names, which you can then change to your own. Take a little time to ponder your company name. It should be memorable; it should be appropriate to your customer group (no point taking on Saga with a company called Crucial Holidays); it should tell people what you do. If you really can't think of a name, have an informal chat with someone in advertising: these people often have a knack for thinking up snappy names. Or was there someone at school who always came up with catchy and probably not very flattering nicknames for people? Chris, my co-writer, once played in a band called Walrus Gumboot, so don't ask him for advice on names.

Once you have your name, of course, get your *domain* name registered as quickly as possible. If you're in high-tech or net-based, .com still seems to be the suffix of choice, but otherwise why not stick to .co.uk?

Patents

If you have a good idea, people will try to steal it. That's a fact of life. At The Instruction Set, we came across a company that had copied our training manuals word for word, even down to our own names in the examples! We actually hired a detective from Pinkerton's to go in and check the story, then threatened to sue them for breach of copyright.

Take a little time to ponder **your company name.** It should be memorable.

The problem is that most theft of intellectual property is rather more subtle than this. Once a piece of plagiarism amends an original work by quite a small amount, it ceases to be legally theft. While I believe there is a role for patent lawyers, especially in areas like biotech, they can cost a lot of money and end up not protecting your intellectual property rights anyway, not through incompetence but because the task is just too difficult.

The best protection of intellectual property rights (IPR) is execution. Not, sadly, of copycats, but in your business: the speed and quality of your delivery. If you are genuinely the first person with an idea, you should be able to bring it to market quickest. That's your initial protection: being there first. Once you are there, make sure you deliver it superbly – on time, in an efficient, friendly, businesslike manner. If you do this, someone who contacts your customers saying 'We do this, too' will be sent away, even if the copycat is cheaper. People don't like changing suppliers and do so only if forced to by continuing poor delivery, ridiculously excessive prices or a step change in the market that renders the product obsolete.

Inevitably, there will come a time when there are a number of copycat products around. Don't be dragged into a price war or endless litigation: keep improving the product and its delivery. At the same time, take obvious precautions against IPR theft by writing © on documents such as course materials, by registering trade marks, and by patenting formulae and key designs.

If I sound vague here, it is because what is 'possible to patent' varies so much from business sector to business sector. If you have experience in the sector in which your start-up is running, you should have a feel for what can and what can't realistically be protected. Be guided by this.

Finally, don't lose sleep. In business, 'ideas are ten a penny' and what really matters is always delivery. Entrepreneurs often think they have

Legal problems almost always arise from **poor communication.**

'totally original ideas' and are terrified that someone will steal them. Actually very few ideas are totally original, and if they are, they may not be good *business* ideas as they might be too far ahead of the market. Leonardo da Vinci didn't get rich out of flying machines. But even if the idea is original and relevant, it is only the beginning of the journey to business success. Remember Edison's remark about genius being 1 per cent inspiration and 99 per cent perspiration.

Litigation

Avoid at all costs! The sad truth about litigation is that once you end up in a court you have already lost. Only the barristers win. And the media if there's a vicar or a soap star involved. If you are on the verge of litigation, stop and ask why. Then sort the problem another way.

Don't litigate, negotiate.

Legal problems almost always arise from poor communication. When you made that first deal, both parties intended to benefit from it. You would get money; your customer would get a product or service that was of use to them. So what has gone wrong? It's time to start negotiating.

Initial deals – and many subsequent deals – are often not based on formal, legally binding contracts. The acceptance is usually verbal. Once a verbal agreement has been reached, you draw up a 'memorandum of understanding' (a.k.a. a 'heads of agreement', a term which will amuse anyone with a naval background). This outlines what you intend to deliver, and how and when and to what standard, and what (and how and when) the customer intends to pay for it. Note that this memorandum also cements the relationship with the client: if a client refuses to agree to this memorandum, this is a real danger signal that they might be 'timewasters', simply trying to gain free market information or up to some internal political game in their company.

Once delivery begins, your sales cornerstone must monitor the process. Is the customer happy? Are things working out as planned? Keep a record of meetings and conversations, so if things do get nasty you have a record of what occurred. (Though even these are of limited use in court.) Remember the story of Theseus, who laid a trail of silk behind him when he went into the Minotaur's labyrinth. The Minotaur, a beast with a bull's head and a man's body and which ate nothing but human flesh, was a lot less scary than most lawyers.

The moment you begin to suspect things aren't going to plan, talk to the client. And listen to the client. Some clients 'try it on', but most don't. Maybe you're not delivering quite what they expected, or the product isn't working as well as expected, or their own needs are changing. Deal with these issues.

Note the importance of keeping the sales team involved with the customer. Businesses selling direct to consumers hand these consumers over from sales to 'customer services' the moment the sale is made. This is very bad practice in a small, business-to-business organization. At Micromuse, a software company I did some work for, the sales team saw all the 'trouble tickets' produced by customer services, even when the company went public and had a huge range of customers.

Many problems occur when customers suggest *changes to a product*. Make sure they know as soon as possible the cost implications of making these changes. Give them a real figure – don't estimate for the sake of speed, ask the relevant technician. Sometimes apparently easy changes can be expensive. Clients sometimes suggest these changes because they are really needed, but not always. The suggestion can be more of an enquiry. I have seen immense ill feeling caused by semi-serious enquiries taken seriously – the customer says in an idle moment 'supposing the widgets were green...'; the supplier goes away and repaints them all, then sends in a bill; the customer refuses to pay.

Note that the customer is fully entitled to change their mind. They're paying. Don't resent these changes, as they are part of the process of making your offer exactly what they want. But always make sure the customer understands the cost implications of their suggestions.

If you do get stuck in one of these traps, negotiate your way out of it. Remember that in good negotiation, both sides win. Negotiators who flatten the opposition win in the short term, but don't expect to see the losers again.

Don't litigate, negotiate.

Other advisors

You will need other professional advice from time to time.

In the early days of The Instruction Set, I was all for getting a mate in to audit the accounts, but the finance cornerstone insisted we call in Coopers and Lybrand (now PricewaterhouseCoopers, and no doubt by the time this book is printed PricewaterhouseCoopersEveryoneElse). Later we had the inevitable visit from the VAT inspector. As you probably know, VAT people have powers that the KGB would envy, and can cause havoc in small businesses. Our inspector simply said, 'Oh, you're audited by Coopers, are you? Fine, we'll have a word with them' and disappeared.

Nice one, Mike...

The basic principle in dealing with outside advisors is 'don't let them charge too much'. Consultants, lawyers, etc. seem to have outrageous cost structures, but this is not your problem. Talk to your mentor and to other entrepreneurs/cornerstones about who offers good and sensibly priced advice. Then go and negotiate with them. 'Deal, deal and deal again,' is Sir Campbell's maxim in these instances. (In the story above, for example, Coopers had a special deal for start-ups.)

It's also worth contacting your local Business Link, who offer a range of free consulting services.

Premises

Getting proper office space is one of the biggest problems faced by seedling enterprises. But tough, it has to be done. Forget all the hype about electronic networks. Working from home is OK for a sole trader, but you are building a team and there needs to be space that belongs to that team and has the unreserved 'feel' of business about it.

By far the best solution to the problem is to try to blag some free office space. This may seem undignified, but there are plenty of organizations with spare space. Try to do some sort of deal with them. Your mentor may well know someone who can help. After all, all you need is a room and a couple of phone lines. Failing this, try adverts in magazines like *Loot*.

Do not worry about the look of the place. When you achieve world domination, then flash offices may be appropriate, but until then, clients visiting your premises don't want to come away thinking they are funding a luxury lifestyle. They want to see commitment, energy and excitement, not fishtanks and Axminster carpets. (I actually worked with an entrepreneur who insisted on having a tank of piranhas

Getting proper office space is one of the biggest problems faced by seedling enterprises.

in reception. And yes, he more than once 'entertained' clients by chucking a goldfish into the tank.)

In fact, wherever possible you should visit the client, not have them visit you. This is not because you've got something to hide but because you can learn a great deal about a client from their premises. Is the office buzzing? If so, they will have plenty of needs; it's up to you to find them. Are the techies really that bright? Watch them at work.

So, as long as there are not too many cockroaches on your potential premises, go for it...

Of course, after a while the free dungeon just becomes too small. But by that time, your business will be ceasing to be a seedling anyway. Once you make the transition from seedling to sapling, you should get some new offices. Proper ones that you rent. I talk more about the delightful process of renting large offices in the next chapter.

Furniture

Your free dungeon probably won't come with furniture. Make some calls, find out the cheapest supplier of second-hand stuff, then hire a van. Make a day of it. All pile into the front – you can even stick a copy of *The Sun* on the dashboard for authenticity – and head off for Fred's Used Office World, Old Kent Road.

Beware of any leases that contain furniture. This is always a hidden way of selling you the stuff at a vastly inflated price. Rent empty premises and fill them yourself.

Getting the phone sorted will be a lot less fun than the furniture. It's a prerequisite of taking free space that there is a working phone line, but the moment you start needing more or better lines, prepare for a war of attrition along the lines of the siege of Stalingrad. All the phone companies seem as bad as each other on this. You just have to keep badgering them. Remind yourself that you aren't asking the phone companies a favour: you're a customer.

The intrapreneur

The intrapreneur, the entrepreneur who does it from inside the big company, has many advantages over the entrepreneur going it alone. Premises? The company will provide them (you may have to find your own Jolly Roger). Finance? The company should set aside a budget for you. Distribution and manufacturing facilities should be available.

But though sections of it might be a little easier, your route to success is essentially the same as the entrepreneur's.

You must find a mentor high in the company – right at the top, if possible. (A corporate mentor is often referred to as your 'sponsor', but their role is the same.) This person will be essential to your project

The **intrapreneur's**
route to success
is the same as
the **entrepreneur's.**

getting off the ground and will continue to champion it when other people in the business start snickering at it – which, believe me, they will, either because it's not working, in which case they'll consider that resources are being wasted, or because it is working and they are jealous.

You must also build a team, four cornerstones, individuals within the company with those core skills but who really believe in, and will bat for, your product. If you can't find all the cornerstones internally, think about finding them outside. They must be highly incentivized – one disadvantage you have over the solo entrepreneur is that you do not have 80 per cent of a business to offer to four talented, loyal team mates. The main incentives you have to offer are a more fun, less corporate working environment and that old corporate goody of 'status within the company'. 'There goes Smith. He was one of the team behind the magic widget.'

Just as the entrepreneur and their cornerstones have to, you must set about refining your product, getting a white paper out once you make your first sale, only drawing up a real business plan when you have some real business to plan.

Conclusion

Remember that evening in the pub? Did you keep the beermat as a souvenir? Frame it and put it on the wall next to the first cheque.

So much has happened since then...

You found a mentor. You got the four cornerstones in place (though Gemma in finance has only just joined full-time). You have trusted, carefully chosen professional advisors, who are offering a special deal because they hope you will stick with them as you grow. You've organized funding – this friend of Sir Everard's had a hundred thousand looking for a home and your first customer paid in advance. You drew up a white paper on the strength of that deal which enabled you to make three more sales. Recently you drew up a real business plan, which features a growth scenario that feels both positive and realistic.

Congratulations!

Now you must understand that your business is about to change its nature. You are about to take on employees, the beginnings of your 'dream team'. You will delegate real responsibility to them: it isn't just five of you plus the receptionist and the gofer, it's about to become a much bigger enterprise. No longer a seedling, but a sapling.

The adventure continues.

the

sapling

enterprise

T he next phase of your business's life covers the period when it grows from a five-person business to one with 20 people on board.

Why 20? I have no idea, but I found it another 'magic number', like five. At The Instruction Set, the whole nature of the company changed after we grew beyond 20. I have seen the same happen in many other businesses since. Governments seem to feel the same: cabinets have contained around 20 individuals since the days of Sir Robert Walpole.

Note that the key dividing line between the phases is number of people in the company, not turnover, profitability or any fancy business ratio. Another indicator of that profound truth that business is fundamentally about people.

In market terms, the fully grown sapling enterprise is a 'boutique'. It serves a niche market; its customers come by personal recommendation (and of course come *back*, again and again). Its style is personal, friendly, deeply committed: everyone in the business shares the vision and is prepared to put in the hours and effort to realize it.

This kind of business can run successfully for years, though a word of warning: I have seen several 'boutiques' become too inward-looking and suddenly find themselves outflanked by new, hungrier opposition, or the market moves on without them.

CEO (Entrepreneur) – source of vision and drive

Sales director	Innovation director	Delivery director	Finance director
3 sales people	2 researchers	5 developers Quality tester Customer support	Admin manager Admin support Accounts assistant

Look at this example of a typical sapling org chart. Naturally, you don't have to follow this pattern slavishly, but it's a useful guide to what the company could well look like once it reaches full sapling size. Note that this growth happens very fast once it begins. The butterfly analogy, with its implications of sudden quantum change, is actually better here: one day you were five plus assistants; six months later, there are 20 in the team. Then you let it plateau out.

The sapling's growth period is a special time. Make sure you take plenty of team photographs at different stages. At The Instruction Set

The key dividing line between

the phases is

number of people

in the company, not turnover,

profitability or any

fancy business ratio.

we took pictures of every person as they joined, and had them pinned up in a 'rogues gallery' in the office, along with a brief description of what they did and an employee number. The latter related to when the individual joined and became very important when the company got big.

Whatever the precise shape of your org chart, one thing is guaranteed. It will be hierarchical. You and your fellow founders aren't just running *and being* the business any longer, you're in charge of people. You're having to hire staff, to pay them salaries and bonuses, to lead them and motivate them.

You have become managers.

➡ 'Help! I wanted to get away from all this boss/underling stuff. All I wanted was to be with a great bunch of mates who believed in this wonderful idea.'

Tough. There's no way a company can stay at five people; it either has to grow or (in the unfortunate and unusual case of a business that makes a few sales but never 'takes off') wither away. Later on, you may have a choice to stay a 'boutique' or to go for 'the big one', but there's no 'grow/no grow' choice at five people. It's grow or die.

So you're managers. Congratulations.

Many people are put off 'management' by images of the old-style 'bastard boss'. But bosses like that have no place in the sapling organization, or in any organization, in my view: if you've got a problem about your loveless upbringing or the size of your penis, go and see a therapist. Other people are put off management by shyness or lack of self-belief. To be honest, they're unlikely to be entrepreneurs or cornerstones, but if you do feel a little diffident about managing others, read on.

Grasp the challenge of management with both hands and really make it a **creative** expression of who you are and what you believe.

The truth is that the basic management skills can be learned. If I had to sum them up in two words, I'd say 'take responsibility', and if I were given a sentence, I'd say: 'Have a clear, well-thought-out formal review process and care about the people below you.'

Enough to be getting on with for the moment? Grasp the challenge of management with both hands and really make it a creative expression of who you are and what you believe. That way you'll succeed, and enjoy it.

Culture and people

As I keep saying, business is ultimately about people. So the most important thing about running a sapling enterprise is getting the *culture* and the *individuals* right.

The culture of the sapling enterprise is tribal. Think chiefs and warriors (modern chiefs and warriors can be female as easily as male). Think close personal relationships. Everyone in the sapling company knows everyone else well. They all get on.

Impossible? No. We did it at The Instruction Set. To be honest, I think that was the main reason for our success. Our product was good, but not that much better than anyone else's. Our people were brilliant.

Building a tribe of 20 people who are both excellent at their work and who get on socially is not easy. It might seem appallingly daunting. But it can be done. Believe in your ability to do it.

At The Instruction Set, we would all go down to the pub most Friday nights. It was great fun and I miss it a lot now. Sometimes the session was totally unstructured (with the only rule that the managers buy the first round and continue to be generous thereafter). Other times we had awards. These awards were, of course, very informal, though behind the informality a lot of thought had gone into who got the awards and why.

There were three basic awards. 'Mini Oscars' went to people who had done particularly special things that month – won a big contract, solved some particularly nagging technical problem, had been particularly praised by a client (or whatever). There was a 'Pranny of the Month' award for some mild balls-up like locking yourself out of your car or spilling coffee all over a report. Finally, 'Unsung Hero' usually went to someone quite junior who'd done something special.

These may sound a bit juvenile, but believe me, they worked. The rather serious accounts assistant glowed with pride on being nominated 'Pranny of the Month': suddenly they had the right not to be so earnest, so quietly, dully perfect. The systems administrator – one of those jobs where you only get noticed when things go wrong – really did appreciate their 'Unsung Hero' award.

In other companies, I've been involved in team-building 'awaydays', getting stuck on mountains or building rafts which, of course, collapse

Our people were
brilliant

halfway over whatever sludge-bottomed piece of water you are supposed to be crossing. The secret of getting the most out of these is to 'mix teams' – in other words have techies and sales people teamed together rather than in watertight 'tech vs sales' competition. Also, show the team you care about these sessions by having them in company time, not at weekends.

A team-building exercise I found particularly useful was role swapping. Get the techies to meet clients. Even better, why not invite your real clients to your team-building sessions? Send the sales staff on a technical course. Efficiency experts might throw up their clipboards in horror at this, but the more everyone in the sapling business understands and appreciates what everyone else does, the better that business will run.

These formal exercises are useful, though to be honest, I think the pub sessions were more effective and enjoyable. And you only get a hangover the next day, not hypothermia or cholera.

Incidentally, the pub is a very good place to spot potential dissent. However good your hiring/culture management, dissenting cliques will spring up occasionally. These need to be nipped in the bud, not by firing dissenters but by talking to the individuals involved and getting to the bottom of what their problem is. Are there three people sitting in one corner, backs turned towards the rest of the team? It sounds obvious, but I've seen it.

Also, it's a sad truth that people do reveal different sides of themselves when they've had a few pints. This can be used cynically, but shouldn't be. If someone expresses dissent over their fifth Foster's, don't take them to task for it next Monday. Talk about it; get the problem sorted.

Office romances may become more apparent in the pub setting, too. Office romances spring up a lot in sapling enterprises. It's a sign that the culture is working: people are really getting close. In an ideal world, they wouldn't get *that* close, but these things happen. Go ahead and celebrate them, with the obvious proviso that the participants' work mustn't suffer.

I'm talking about romances between equals, of course. Unmarried equals, preferably. I know of companies where senior people have abused their position to pursue subordinates, and it is very damaging to 'tribe' morale. If you really do decide that the accounts assistant is the love of your life, then he or she will have to leave the firm. If you just fancy a casual fling with them, go and take a cold shower and act more maturely. (This may seem harsh, but it's called self-discipline. Note that it also protects you from the 'VP vampire' phenomenon, common in the States and making its way over here, where a junior seduces a senior, acts so unreasonably that the senior is forced to end the entanglement, then hits them with a huge lawsuit.)

The truth is that office romance is out for the founding team. You can't pursue juniors, and romances with other cornerstones create terrible imbalances of power in the boardroom.

Get everyone
in the organization
involved in
recruitment.

Recruitment

Recruitment is probably the single most important issue for the sapling company. So get everyone in the organization involved in it. Incentivize the bringing in of good people. 'I've got this mate who'd be just perfect for that job. I know they're not happy where they are at the moment.' Brilliant!

A good culture really helps here. If your staff think that working for you is the best game in town, they will be eager to get people they like on board. At the same time they will think carefully about who they bring in. Think teenage kids and gangs and you won't be far wrong.

As the entrepreneur or a cornerstone, you are still in overall charge of the hiring process, however. You can't rely on new team members bringing in mates; you should always be looking for solutions to staffing problems yourself. Use contacts unashamedly. Personal recommendations; people you've seen do a good job; friends. Our merito-cratic business ethos frowns on this approach: images of old school ties and strange Masonic handshakes come to mind. But for the sapling enterprise, trust and enthusiasm are key qualities, and it is simple common sense to look for these where you would look in ordinary life, among people you meet and like.

The only caveat is to watch out for cronyism by the entrepreneur. As you know, entrepreneurs are single-minded (to put it tactfully) and may try to surround themselves with sycophants, the type you see hanging round pop stars telling them they're cool every ten minutes. The best way to avoid this is to make each director responsible for hiring within their department. Giving everyone in the team a veto (see below) is another valuable and effective safeguard.

The alternative to hiring via contact is hiring by interview. Straight, open, fair – and highly problematic until you're a much bigger company with a proper HR department and proper HR procedures. The interview process may be open and fair, but not all applicants are. Early on at The Instruction Set, we hired a couple of people who performed brilliantly at interview and came with good references, but who turned out not to be up to the job. We found out one had been fired from his previous job and had been given a good reference because the referee was too embarrassed to tell the truth.

We stopped hiring by this method and never looked back. Trust your judgement. And that of your colleagues.

When you do decide to hire somebody, introduce them to the rest of the team. Not just to the entrepreneur and the other cornerstones, but to everyone in the business. And if *anyone* expresses misgivings, don't hire the person. This sounds draconian, but it works. We began doing it that way at The Instruction Set and only lost two people after that. It's the intuition thing again. Trust it.

The new arrival should be on a three-month trial period. You should put some time into your diary two months into that period to talk with your fellow cornerstones about this person. Are they fitting in? Are they delivering what they said they would? The former is the biggest problem. 'Brilliant but disruptive' people cause more trouble than they're worth. Look out for signs of a poor temperamental fit:

➡ rude to junior staff;

➡ poor timekeeping;

➡ obsession with status;

➡ long personal calls or lots of time on the internet on irrelevant sites.

After three months, if they are not 'gelling', it's time for them to go.

But pick people well, get everyone to vet them, motivate them once they arrive, and you won't have to dismiss people. They won't leave, either, unless a major change of personal circumstances forces them to. To me a 'hire and fire' culture is the opposite of good business practice, and the fact that it's so common in the City makes me genuinely suspicious of the City (along with its role in the dot-com bubble). Are City institutions really as clever as they make out, or just lucky to have access to ridiculously large flows of money on which they'd have to be idiots not to make a turn?

Dismissal

If you *do* have to dismiss somebody, it is infinitely better that they leave on good terms rather than bad. Most sapling enterprises operate in quite small business areas and you don't want enemies out there gunning for you. Also, 'friendly dismissal' is in keeping with the tribal atmosphere of trust.

How can this be achieved? By making the dismissal process open and unambiguously fair.

There are two main reasons for dismissal. One is simple failure to do the job properly, the other is misconduct. In both cases, there are correct procedures to follow.

When someone has to go because of poor performance, there should be a clearly understood pathway, which forms part of the appraisal process (a section on appraisal follows). For misconduct, staff should get a verbal warning, then a written warning, before being dismissed. Some people say this is too soft and cite silly examples of giving people verbal warnings for coming into work one morning and smashing up the computers (or the computer operators) with an axe. These counter-examples are not realistic: stick to this procedure.

The most difficult dismissal is of someone who has the ability and has been trying their best but has been underperforming due to circumstances beyond their control. Examples: a partner or child has a life-threatening illness; the individual is hit by illness or depression. The first thing to do is to try to get help for them. If this doesn't work, there may have to be a parting of the ways, at least temporarily.

It is best to have two meetings with the person being dismissed. The first is relatively brief. Explain that they have not achieved what was hoped, run through the formal aspects (warnings, missed targets), ask them if they really feel at home in their work. They may well be very honest about this, as they are secretly guilty at letting the rest of the tribe down (though for some people, problems are always somebody else's fault). Then break the bad news. Offer a good severance package. Avoid personal criticism in all cases.

Appraisal lies at the

heart of

good management.

Some 'dismissees' threaten to get in lawyers. Fine. If you have followed my advice, you have stuck to both law and agreed company procedure and thus have nothing to fear. Usually these threatened lawyers disappear once the departing individual gets a cost estimate from them.

There should be a second meeting, the exit interview, a while later. The person leaves, takes a break, comes to terms with what has happened, then comes back to tie up any loose ends. Agree to differ on any contentious points. Finalize severance agreements. Make the parting amicable.

Some enlightened companies actually try to find jobs for ex-employees – Accenture (formerly Andersen Consulting) does this, with the result that it has friends in high places all over the business world.

Appraisal

I've mentioned appraisal above but I want to look at it in greater depth as it lies at the heart of good management. It should happen every six months: you sit down with each team member and look at what they have done in that six months, at what they can learn from it, at what you expect from them in the next six months. At the same time, it's a good opportunity to get some feedback about how *you* are perceived, and to talk to the individual about the company in general, where it's going and how you see their role in that development.

If someone fails to meet the goals set six months ago, the best question to ask is what you can do to help them get it right next time. 'What do you need to do the job better?' is an infinitely better question than 'Why?', which just puts people on the defensive. Usually they will tell you what they need. Go with this, using your intelligence and intuition. For example, a sales person says they've got a horrible client list. Is this an excuse or a real reason? If it's the latter, find them some better ones.

If their answer feels like an excuse, probe deeper. Sales staff often complain about props like the brochure, but this is rarely the problem: selling is about preparation, confidence, rapport, not brochures. Go with them on a visit, try to spot what they are doing wrong. It will often be something very obvious. If so, stay cool, point out the error and let them learn from the experience.

The same is true of technical staff. Work alongside them, see what they're doing wrong, help them sort it out.

Failure to meet a realistic target can be a signal of a weakness that can easily be remedied. If you don't set targets it's amazing how much you can miss.

Finally, remember that if there's an individual that you (and the rest of the team) really like and who really likes the company but who is underperforming, consider whether they might be of use elsewhere in the company. You are well shot of mediocrity and lack of interest, but passion that hasn't quite found its best medium of expression is like unrefined gold. Work on it.

Leadership

I said earlier that you have now become managers, but what you have really become is *leaders*.

Does that sound better?

Some of you will thrill at this thought. Others may shiver, as thoughts of Chairman Mao or Orwell's 'Big Brother' come into your heads. Forget these negative images. The truth is that leadership is a wonderful, soul-expanding experience – if done in the right spirit, which is positive, adventurous and humane. People will love you for providing really good leadership.

Leadership

is a wonderful, soul-expanding experience – if done in the right spirit, which is **positive, adventurous** and **humane.**

As a leader, your two main jobs are strategic and motivational. You have to work out where the business is going and decide firmly on the best way of getting there and get everybody else heading in that direction, too. In the sapling enterprise, strategy is the lesser of these two challenges. I talk a little about it later, but first, and most important, is...

Motivation

What does actually motivate people? That's a classic 'how long is a piece of string?' question, as there are so many different sorts of people in the world. But we are only looking at the kind of people you need and who will flourish in the sapling enterprise. Your 'dream team'. I have a great deal of experience with such people and know what they want.

Hint, it's not money. Not most of all, anyway. In descending order it is the following.

Respect

Self- and peer respect. They like the people they work with. They respect them and are respected by them. Outside working hours, they tell their friends they are working for your company and expect those friends to be pleased for them, impressed, envious, or all of these things.

Making a difference

Many employees of sapling enterprises come from big organizations where they have felt swamped and irrelevant. They want to be involved in the making of decisions, and they want to know that their decisions and actions have a real effect. This is a gentler but still powerful version of the entrepreneur's passion for changing the world.

Challenge

Sapling employees are there for a challenge, to stretch themselves, to learn and grow. There is plenty of opportunity for this in saplings: there are always more things to do than people to do them. So if anyone has the balls to say 'Let me try', unless it's outrageously inappropriate, let them.

Advancement

If you're really into scaling ladders, you will probably go and join a big corporation and scheme your way to an office with *two* telephones and a carpet one millimetre thicker than the bloke next door's. Life in a sapling enterprise is more about the challenge of the job than getting 'vice president' on your business card. But there will be opportunities for advancement if the sapling grows into a mighty oak, and some people join sapling organizations with this clearly in mind.

Money

Of course it does matter, so pay people as well as you can afford. Give bonuses, too, but *not* individual ones, whatever any books on management, experts you meet in pubs (etc.) tell you. It simply isn't true that you can pay people wildly different amounts of money and they won't find out. They will, and the discovery of huge differentials will breed arrogance, demotivation, distrust. Individual bonuses go right against the tribal, team environment that drives sapling enterprises. You are all in this together, remember? Team bonuses are, of course, good things; given to everyone, based on the performance of the tribe as a whole.

I believe that everyone's salary and bonuses should be public knowledge. The sort of people you want to employ in sapling organizations aren't envious. They're quite happy for someone in the organization to be earning £200,000 p.a., provided they think that person is adding an appropriate amount of value to the team effort. Post salaries on the company intranet – why not? If anyone comes and asks why they are 'underpaid', explain why, and what they have to do to get paid better. And if your £200,000 person is clearly useless – I've worked with people getting twice this amount who seemed to bring nothing to the party at all – then the more embarrassed and humiliated they feel at this, the better.

Such a policy encourages openness. It discourages overgenerous 'golden hellos' to people (often pals of the entrepreneur).

Stock options are another bone of contention. They're a great idea, in theory, but the idea was so abused in the dot-com bubble that I now

I believe that everyone's **salary and bonuses** should be public knowledge.

put them in my personal Room 101, along with arrogant MBAs, greedy VCs (etc.). In my view, stock options in sapling companies should be regarded as worthless. If you are seeking a job in such a company and they offer you a tiny salary but plenty of options, ignore the options and ask yourself whether you are prepared to work for these people for the salary they are offering. Your answer may be 'yes' because they are great people with a great product, which is fine. If the answer is 'no', walk away.

Sapling stock options are usually illusions. As the company gets bigger and bigger, your stake does not grow but shrinks because more and more options get allocated. In some cases early-granted options mysteriously disappear altogether, via some arcane refinancing package. It becomes legally possible but, given legal costs, actually impossible to get these options back.

Entrepreneurs can start treating options like royal patronage, handing them out to all and sundry. This dilutes existing stakes and can lead to a situation where the company effectively has to cheat people. I know of one entrepreneur who promised more than 100 per cent of his business in stock options!

There is a proper use for stock options, and I talk about this in the next chapter.

To return to our 'hierarchy of motivations', the least important ones are *security* and *work environment*.

Security is rather despised by the young go-getters who join sapling enterprises. Note, however, that older employees start worrying about it. Older people can be very valuable in sapling teams, so bear this change of priority in mind.

As regards environment, The Instruction Set started in a basement. By the standard of some start-ups, this would have embarrassed Louis XIV with its luxury. You should now be moving to new premises (see page 104), but they still won't be those marble-halled corporate temples the entrepreneur dreams of.

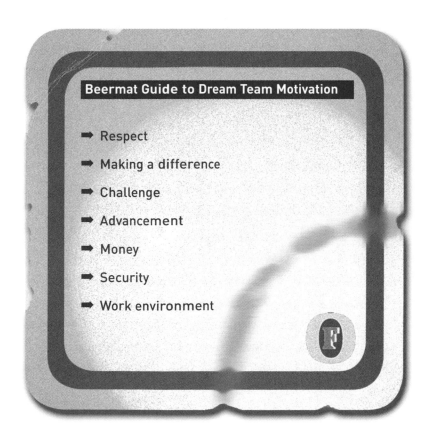

Beermat Guide to Dream Team Motivation

➡ Respect

➡ Making a difference

➡ Challenge

➡ Advancement

➡ Money

➡ Security

➡ Work environment

There really are only 20 of you, and it's **you** against the world.

And it's bloody marvellous.

So that is the hierarchy of needs in the sapling enterprise. It's not that different from Maslow's classic actually, with achievement and self-expression at the top and security and surroundings at the bottom.

Long after The Instruction Set had been sold, I did some work with Insights Ltd, a company that specialized in motivation. I learned a lot of things I wish I'd known when I was building my business (although we did get it largely right, by instinct, or by the desire to work with people we liked and to spend time in pubs with them).

Insights Ltd dealt with organizations of all sizes, but its message was particularly suited to the sapling enterprise. It was run by Will Carling, the former England rugby captain. He and a few chosen sportsmen and women made a good business out of applying lessons and techniques from professional sport to the workplace.

The tribal sapling enterprise is the ideal place to use these techniques. The number of people involved is about the same as a sports team. The age profile of sapling employees is similar to that of most sports teams: young, energetic, 'up for it'. (I'll discount the amazing cricket XI I play for once a year, whose tail begins when No. 3 comes to the wicket, and where the older players such as myself stay in one deep fielding position all afternoon.) Sapling business really is a sports-team game in a way that seedling isn't (too small) and the massive corporation, despite the endless corporate flannel about 'teambuilding', can never be.

There really are only 20 of you, and it's you against the world. And it's bloody marvellous, believe me!

The great captains motivate their players in a number of ways.

Understanding the individual

Sportsmen and women may seem super-competent, but they vary as much in temperament as employees. Some are plagued with lack of confidence: it's their undeservedly low self-image that keeps them practising and practising. Others have booming, overconfident egos: success comes to them because they know it will. Out on the field it may not be clear which person has which self-image. Give them the wrong kind of motivation and it becomes apparent at once.

Mike Brearley was arguably England's greatest cricket captain. He led England to victory in the famous 1981 Headingley test by bowling out Australia, who needed a mere 130 to win, for 111. The man who did the damage was Bob Willis. When he put Willis on to bowl, Brearley had a few words with him, along the lines of: 'I know you're getting a bit past it, Bob, but I guess as you're in the team you ought to have a couple of overs. Don't bowl *too* badly, though.'

Other team members required totally different motivation. Apparently tough, no-nonsense Yorkshireman Geoff Boycott needed regular reassurance. Ultra-competitive Ian Botham needed to know the skipper wasn't trying to rival him. Derek Underwood, that most technically minded of bowlers, needed a lot of listening to and consultation about all the details of tactics. No two individuals' 'motivation buttons' are the same, and it is the job of the leader to know exactly where their team's are.

It is interesting to speculate how many people who appear to be under-performers are actually people whom nobody has taken the trouble to work out how to motivate. Of course, ideally we should all be self-motivators – if you are an entrepreneur, intrapreneur or cornerstone, you will be.

Not slagging off failure but learning from it

There's no point in getting at people for their failures. If somebody goofs, the need is for them, and the rest of the team, to learn from that mistake. Success should be dwelt on, failure shouldn't.

Blame cultures encourage people to put their own safety before the welfare of the group, to score cheap points off one another, and generally to avoid risk. Not exactly what you want in an entrepreneurial business, or a sports team whose job it is to go out and win.

Note that our 'Pranny of the Month' ceremony in the pub was always carefully set up to be in a light, humorous spirit – a spirit of forgiveness and inclusion rather than of blame and exclusion.

Celebrating success

This gets drilled into sports teams, which is why you see macho footballers kissing and hugging each other after a goal. Your team achievements should be celebrated too, with days out, bottles of champagne at the office, meals, trips to concerts, movies. You are effectively writing the story of your company's success here, and the more clearly that story is embedded in everybody's minds via happy memories, the better.

Giving praise

Individual success should be celebrated, too – in public, which multiplies the motivational value of the praise many times. It's extraordinary how seldom people get praise from some bosses, even when the boss genuinely reckons that the work has been excellent. But there is no better way of motivating people (see 'respect' above). Giving praise also sends out a general message: this is a place where excellence is encouraged and celebrated. In Britain, we're not very good at this. Good old mediocrity, 'not rocking the boat', has been the norm. It's important to break down this attitude and to understand that it does not need to be replaced by rampant individualism but by positive, enthusiastic teamwork.

Stay positive

This is hugely important. Leaders have to look positive. Will Carling tells the story of how, just before a crucial England–Scotland game, he was spotted wandering around the team hotel, deep in thought. It wasn't that he was worried, just that he wanted to think of something original to say to the team. Observers misinterpreted this and thought he'd given up on the game. Gloom set in. Until Will realized what had happened, he was baffled by this sudden change of morale; once he had spotted the cause, he was able to address the problem. England went on to win.

Being visible

Visibility is also important in big companies: you won't be able to hide later on. A similar story to Will's comes from Next PLC. The CEO came out of the boardroom one day after excellent reports all round, pondering the next move. As he walked down the corridor, lost in thought, staff spotted his expression and panic set in among them. 'The boss is upset!' 'Something's gone terribly wrong!' 'How many are going to be laid off?' 'Bet you 1,000.' 'More like 2,000 probably.' Morale nose-dived and it took a meeting of head office staff to get it back again.

As a leader you must give off 'positive vibes'. All the time. Whatever is happening in your personal life, or to the company for that matter. This

As a leader you **must** give off **'positive vibes'**. All the time.

does not mean 'tell lies about the state of the business', of course. It means stay positive and show it, all the time.

Generating enthusiasm

This is a job for the entrepreneur and it really is a gift. You can't learn how to do this really effectively (though like all 'emotional intelligence' skills, you can improve those gifts that you have). Entrepreneurs do it naturally, their enthusiasm bubbling out all over the place and their commitment showing that they really mean it.

Leading from the front

Showing you mean it means leading from the front, it means being seen to be working as hard and as smart as your brightest employee. The old-style corporate manager who did a lot of 'work' on the golf course or over a long lunch may well still have a role in a big company – contacts are kept alive this way – but this is not a style that suits the sapling enterprise. Watch Martin Johnson lead the England rugby team from the scrum; watch Roy Keane haring up and down the field at Old Trafford, always involved, always passionate. The other players give 110 per cent because their leaders do.

Setting goals

Leaders *set goals*. Goal setting is about having a vision of where an individual can get to, and about understanding the steps they have to take to get there. Well-set goals 'plot a path' to success via a series of challenging but achievable milestones.

Here's a great story about goal setting. Adrian Moorhouse concluded that to win gold at the Seoul Olympics he needed to swim 100 metres in 1.02 minutes. At the time, he was taking 1.04 minutes. The Olympics were less than a year away. He actually set himself the target of swimming the distance in one hundredth of a second less *every day*. By the Olympics, he had met his target and duly went out and won.

Will Carling used to say that the captain's job was to 'create an environment where people could succeed'. That is as good a summary of the leader's job as I can think of.

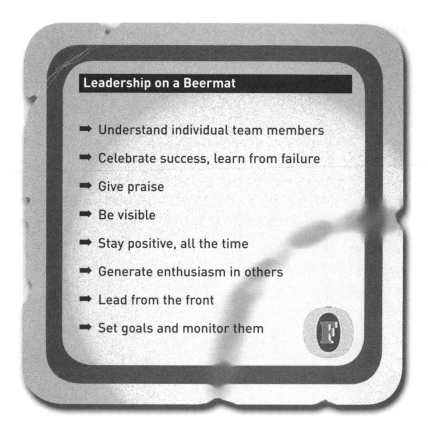

Leadership on a Beermat

➡ Understand individual team members

➡ Celebrate success, learn from failure

➡ Give praise

➡ Be visible

➡ Stay positive, all the time

➡ Generate enthusiasm in others

➡ Lead from the front

➡ Set goals and monitor them

Strategic leadership

I said that leaders have two functions, strategic and motivational. In the sapling organization, the latter is more important than the former.

There is not too much complex strategic thinking to be done at this stage in the business's life. The aim, simply, is to grow. The means are:

➡ happy, motivated people;

➡ carefully controlled costs;

➡ delighted customers.

Not too much strategic wizardry there. At this stage you *shouldn't* be innovating that much: you have your core product, and though you will find yourself tailoring it to particular customers, you will not be altering it radically until you hear the 'growl' of the competition.

Business magazines are full of articles on creativity, the need for perpetual innovation and so on. But the sapling stage is an odd period when these actually don't matter that much. Your product must have been innovative to have got this far: right now creative thinking is about finding uses and markets for it.

The entrepreneur will still be thinking strategically, anyway. Entrepreneurs do. The cornerstones' job is to downplay this and keep the enterprise focused on the job in hand. When you go for growth and become a mighty oak, then strategy will come into its own.

Incidentally, I find it intriguing that strategy-speak often resorts to the imagery of war. There's a whole sub-genre of books that wheel out classic military thinkers like Sun Zi ('Sun Tzu' in old-fashioned spelling) or Clausewitz and reinterpret what they teach for the business market. This may be relevant to great corporations, but I believe strongly that the sports field is an infinitely better metaphor and inspiration for the sapling business.

Sapling sales

I have talked about the aspirations that the seedling sales cornerstone should have: a portfolio of 10 to 15 customers, with 20 prospects in their sights. Of course, this is the ideal state of the sapling organization.

My model may appear too high-tech or service-orientated ('It's all right for people running Unix training courses, but we make widgets'), but I don't believe it is. Sapling manufacturers overwhelmingly sell to other businesses, either to other manufacturers or to big retailers. If so, they are in exactly the same position as a high-tech company or service provider – you have big customers, and your job is to keep them convinced you meet their real needs better than anyone else.

For example, if you have a wonderful mineral spring in your back garden, you could bottle the water and sell it in the local market. If you want to build the business, however, this strategy won't work – you need an intermediary who will get the water to many more people. Work out who this might be. Retailers? Offices with thirsty workers? Caterers? Then think about how, in each case, you could add value to your product. Examples: providing the thirsty office with a dispenser which you undertake to fill regularly; providing the caterer with special bottles with 'Ethel and Fred, Silver Wedding' on. The retailer is the hardest nut to crack here, as they are ruthless with suppliers. But all the more need for you to convince them that your water is special. Nobody, not even the stingiest supermarket chain, is above the laws of the market. If it were suddenly found to be the only water in the world with the same properties as Viagra, you would have retailers queuing outside your gates begging you to let them sell your product (as well as wanting a sip, no doubt).

The point of all this is that selling in the sapling organization is still about meeting the needs of a relatively small number of actual and potential customers. The time for armies of reps, call centres, etc. is still a long way away. Remember that in sapling selling nothing beats personal contact. Your sales cornerstone was selected because they were likeable, confident and a good listener. They should be using those traits now, to instigate, build and cement a continuing relationship with those customers. They should meet the client at least once a month and be in touch by e-mail once a week.

These 'nudge' e-mails should be short and offer real value to the reader, information that may not change the world but that is relevant and

Remember that
in sapling selling nothing beats
personal contact.

interesting. 'Did you hear about XYZ's deal with BT?' 'Have you heard Jane Doe has left ABC?' If you can phrase it as a question, that increases involvement.

Telemarketing is also a useful tool at this point, maintaining your database of reserve potential clients (the 100 or so queuing up behind your 20 lead potential customers). 'Is Bill Smith still the purchasing director at ABC Grommets, and has his e-mail changed?' It's amazing how much information these calls can yield if the person at the other end of the line is chatty. If they're not, get the info and move on.

In dealing with new business, it is a good idea to get the entrepreneur involved early on so that they can work some of their charm and passion on the customer. Then get them out of the loop or they'll start meddling. Towards the end of the negotiation, when things are getting to the 'nitty gritty' stage of bargaining over delivery times, payment schedules and so on, get the finance cornerstone to negotiate with the customer's purchasing director. At the end, the entrepreneur can reappear and thank the customer for their business.

Remember that in your real business plan you had 10 customers in mind. When you actually have 10 customers (they may not be the originally planned 10), then you have leapt another hurdle. Well done!

And when these 10 customers are delighted with you, that's yet another hurdle overcome.

Where to look for quality leads? You can't beat promoting conferences and seminars. Such events are good general exposure for the company and can be an excellent showcase for particular products. Make sure the events offer real benefits: get good external speakers and have really useful information on offer. That way people associate you with quality. You can also charge for the conferences and still get a decent turnout: 100 people is ideal, big enough to make the room look full, but small enough so that you can get your people to talk to each delegate. Half a day is long enough for most people's attention span. Offer a nice buffet lunch as a closer, and a free afternoon demonstration of your product at work. Anyone who stays behind for this is a serious potential customer. Offer them a free seminar at their site.

These targeted client seminars are the most effective account development tool I know, the equivalent to 100 sales visits in one day.

Telesales people are ideal for promoting these conferences. Use them. Of course, you should avoid telesales *direct to consumers*, which will make people hate you. ('Hello, I'm Darren, and I know you're just about to sit down to a candlelit dinner with your partner but I wonder if you'd like to talk about double glazing for 10 minutes instead.')

I love sapling enterprises because I'm a salesman and because the fact is that *sales drive sapling enterprises*. Market instinct and technology drive the seedling; marketing and delivery drive the mighty oak; but the sapling grows by the oldest business art of all: good selling.

Problems and advisors

The seedling company needs a few good advisors, and the same is true of the sapling. In both enterprises, there is a premium on vision, passion and commitment. This is as it should be, but it brings the potential downside of myopia. We all have a great capacity for seeing

Problems in sapling organizations nearly all come from quite simple sources.

things as we want to, or as we expect to, which makes the objective eye of the trusted outside professional of enormous value.

However spot-on your vision and however masterly your execution, something will go wrong at some time. Probably several things will go wrong at several times, and every now and then several things will go wrong at once. The first thing to do is 'ask the troops'. Get the opinions of the people at the coal face: sales and technical staff. Together, have a careful think about what has gone wrong and why. Problems in sapling organizations nearly all come from quite simple sources. Here are some scenarios, and what to do if they arise.

➡ **You run out of cash.** Get selling, fast! I have been told more than once: 'If you don't sell something tomorrow, we're going broke.' It certainly concentrates the mind. However, it shouldn't really happen. The finance cornerstone should be watching cash flow like a hawk. They should have an imaginary timetable of 'how many months till the closing-down party', and when that total gets low, everyone should be put on red alert. Sell more, spend less!

➡ **Costs out of control.** That's the other thing the finance cornerstone should be fixated with. Get pruning fast.

➡ **Too many products.** This can happen if you over-customize, making sales unprofitable. An issue for the sales cornerstone. Also a very common problem. At the time of writing, I'm wondering whether internet giant amazon.com isn't lurching down that dangerous road of trying to be everything to everybody. Successful businesses hit known, clearly defined markets hard.

➡ **Downturn in market.** A popular excuse for failure, but a bad one. Great companies survive the inevitable ups and downs of markets. You are building a great company. The obvious answer to this problem is to 'work harder and smarter'. But also consider that market downturns can be opportunities. Are some of your less fit competitors going to vanish? Supplies – and more importantly, quality people – will be cheaper.

➡ **Rival produces a better product.** Make an even better one! You have some leeway: your customers won't change at once. They like you; what they want to hear from you is 'Yes, that is a great product. But we're going to beat it – just watch.' It's also true that amazing new products can develop glitches. Don't panic, just put your innovation team on overdrive.

➡ **Rival produces an 'order of magnitude' better product.** (For example, what happened to Hoover when Dyson's cleaner came out.) Actually, your response should be the same as the above. Make a better one. Don't indulge in 'dirty tricks', trying to sabotage the new product, both because you should have better ethics than that and because when the truth comes out, people will despise you for it.

➡ **A rival tries to buy market share.** Talk to your customers. Try to find out whether your rival has a real cost advantage (if they have, then try to match it) or if the price-cutting is pure aggression. In most markets, buying share is a short-term strategy that often rebounds on the price-cutter. Customers know perfectly well what the outcome will be – a near-monopolist who will suddenly turn round and ramp prices back up – and are distrustful of this kind of ploy. But they need reassurance from you. Their FD has been muttering about costs. They will probably buy a few rival widgets and try them out. Your product should be better, so should see off the opposition. Of course, if you have a product that's worse and more expensive, you shouldn't be in the market anyway!

➡ **A key person in your business wants out.**   Let them go. Talk to your mentor about finding a quality replacement. This is more common a problem in 'mighty oak' companies, and I talk more about this issue in that section.

If you have been through all the possible obvious solutions, talking them over with the team, your mentor, your non-execs and anyone else you respect and who is prepared to give you free advice, and you're still baffled, maybe it is time to call in outsiders. As at the seedling stage, don't let them overcharge. I've been appalled by some of the work I've seen from big-name consultants, not because it was bad but because of the price tag attached.

I also hate consultancy work, with any price ticket, that's in fluent management-ese. The philosopher Wittgenstein said: 'Everything that can be said can be said clearly.' And that should be the motto of all business communication.

Finance

Just as at the seedling stage, *avoid external finance* if you can. The best way to finance a sapling business is through cash flow.

➡ Keep the orders flowing.

➡ Keep the customers paying on time.

➡ Keep outgoings as low as possible.

Bank loans to cover working capital, and which are not secured against your house, are pretty benign sources of capital, so don't fight shy of them.

However exciting your product, **bright, motivated people** will **not** come and work for you for peanuts.

Growing companies cannot afford to throw money around. The absurd pantomime of boo.com should be a lesson to us all – though note that the founders were encouraged to spend money like water by their City investors, under the mistaken idea that it would 'raise profile' (or rather the mistaken idea that such a raised profile would automatically bring in business. Riding a unicycle along the M25 dressed in a clown suit will raise your profile but is unlikely to make you rich).

At the same time, of course, beware of false economies. Outmoded technology, inefficient support staff, crummy business cards (or no business cards at all). There is always a fine line to be drawn. The best way to draw it is to make the people spending the money have to convince a sceptical financial cornerstone that the expenditure really is necessary. If they make a good enough case, a cheque is drawn. If they don't make out a good enough case, they get a reasonable explanation.

One area where economies are almost always false is people. However exciting your product, bright, motivated people will not come and work for you for peanuts. Pay a little over the going rate and monitor their progress carefully to make sure they are delivering value for money.

Continue to move heaven and earth to finance your business from cash flow.

PR/media

Establish contact with those freelance journalists whose names appear regularly in the relevant *specialist* press. If you have a story, pitch it to these people who, if they like it, will pitch it to the publication. Most press releases sent directly to publications go straight into the bin.

If you have a well-known customer who is happy with your work, see whether their PR department will work with you on a case study. These are the stories that the publications really want – not dull product releases but genuine customer stories of problems solved (by your product, of course!).

But don't worry too much about PR. Sapling enterprises don't really need the media. As a sapling, your main customer relationships are still personal: no amount of press coverage can make up for poor one-to-one relationships with individual customers.

If by any chance you do get a piece in the media and a flood of orders comes in as a result, is that a win? Only if you can handle them all, which is unlikely. What you need is as regular a flow of orders as possible, gained through personal contact and recommendation.

The mass media have the added disadvantage of being obsessed with building people up then knocking them down. Any media star has been through this appalling mill. Pop stars like Geri Halliwell seem to be able to emerge out of it with a grin on their face, but most people don't. Entrepreneurs like Sir Clive Sinclair, who was made a hero for the ZX then knocked down when the C5 appeared, and Keith McCullagh, whose media image soared and plummeted with British Biotech's share price, would really have been better off if they'd never seen a reporter. As would Will Carling, though as a sportsman he had little choice in the matter. You do have that choice, and should exercise it in favour of caution and quietly getting on with your job.

Note that earlier I said that leaders should be 'visible'. I meant, of course, visible within the world of the organization and its customers, not to the sensation-seeking world out there.

Naturally, one person will disagree violently with this section: the entrepreneur. They can't wait to get into the press, specialist, national, whatever, telling the world about themselves and what they've achieved. Steer them towards the specialist press. This is less glamorous (so the entrepreneur might get bored), more responsible and better targeted.

Later on, when the enterprise is more corporate, mass awareness becomes important and PR comes into its own. 'Entrepreneur super-stars' can flourish then – think of Richard Branson, Anita Roddick or Victor Kiam. But even these people have a rough ride.

Law

Here again, there is no real difference between seedling and sapling. Don't take on specialist legal staff. Keep legal expenditure down by using boilerplate contracts. Above all, stay well away from the courts.

Now you have more contracts to watch, there is more opportunity for things to go wrong, so stay alert and keep talking to your customers.

Employment contracts will start to matter. The boilerplate rule still applies: keep them simple. And remember that, while contracts are necessary, the most important part of an employment agreement is unwritten and 'psychological': you're recruiting members of a tribe, and legal niceties are largely irrelevant to this.

Premises

I said that one of the first things you do as a sapling company is move to your own premises. This is a special moment.

Finding the premises is rather less special.

For starters, it brings you into contact with commercial estate agents, another candidate for my Room 101. Arguably, they're the worst of the lot, as they tell lies. I know I'll get letters from the professional body whingeing, but I'm sorry, it's happened to me. When The Instruction Set was looking for premises, a commercial estate agent found 'just the place'. 'Look, there's even training going on there at the moment!' We nearly signed the lease, until we found out that the current occupants were operating illegally, and the premises only had planning permission for light industrial use.

Estate agents will also send you to ridiculously inappropriate properties, presumably to convince the property's owner that they are on the case. I'm sorry to be negative about a group of people who come in for a lot of stick, but they deserve it. If any commercial estate agents are reading this – clean up your act!

The entrepreneur also becomes totally infuriating while you are seeking premises. Premises are an expression of the business, and the business is an expression of their ego, so they immediately drop all the useful work they were doing in staff motivation and business development and set off on a personal mission to find the perfect office. They abandon their desk, their mobile is permanently switched off, you're about to send out a search party, when they waltz into the office saying they've found exactly what the business needs. This will turn out to be horrifically expensive and, amazingly, a five-minute walk from their own home, though impossible to get to for everyone else.

There's only a little you can do to mitigate this. Chaining the entrepreneur to their desk might work, but they'll escape through the window when you let them go to the loo. The only practical solution is to get someone whom the entrepreneur trusts to draw up a short list of properties, then send the entrepreneur to look round these.

Note that the comments I made in the previous chapter about simple premises are still valid. The entrepreneur may want something grand, but your customers won't respect you for it. Stay simple.

When the entrepreneur has decided – and it really is best to let them decide – get your lawyers onto the lease. The cornerstones should visit, too, but nobody else, or you'll get endless arguments about commuting distances.

Someone will have the lovely job of ensuring the place fits health and safety regulations. These need to be taken seriously, as environmental health officers can close you down if you are breaching these regulations. You also need to consider security. Think burglar for a moment, and imagine how you might get in. Talk to the local police. You must have an effective and appropriate alarm system, though this will inevitably cause trouble at some time, going off at three o'clock one morning for no reason.

At the moment, the biggest security problem for small businesses is laptops. It's almost impossible to police a busy start-up enterprise, where people are always coming and going. However many badges your receptionist pins on incomers, someone will sneak in sometime. So make sure your people lock their laptops away if there's not going to be anyone else in their office for a while, and make sure they always lock laptops away at night. The last person home should lock up any stray laptops, too. You can get laptop insurance, and this is worth shopping around for.

When laptops do disappear, the hardware is only part of the loss – ask MI5, who seem to make a habit of leaving them on trains or in unlocked cars. You should guard against theft (and computer-borne disasters) by backing up all your machines at least once a week. Do it every day if you can. Get a good systems administrator to ensure this happens.

The entrepreneur may want **something** grand, but your customers won't respect you for it. Stay simple

But don't lose sleep over security. Get the basics right, and get on with business.

When you finally move in to your new home, make a party out of it. Have all the staff line up outside the entrance and have photos taken. Lay on some champagne and food inside, even bring music (don't leave this to the postboy who says he's got an amazing sound system and turns out to like nothing but Death Metal).

Celebrate! This place, for all its drawbacks, is going to be very, very special.

Marketing

Marketing is an often-misunderstood word. It is not a euphemism for dodgy large-scale selling; it is a proper commercial discipline that involves looking at huge ranges of consumers and breaking them down into reasonably predictable groups that have similar purchase/consumption patterns. As I said in the 'selling' section, you still aren't really doing marketing.

Nonetheless, marketing and communications companies may try to convince you that you need an expensive brochure. You don't. You need a clear vision of what you do and how that benefits customers, and you need likeable, efficient sales people who understand that vision and communicate it, person to person.

Neither do you really need expensive market data. You're not attacking a whole market yet.

You will need to do marketing when the company grows beyond the sapling stage, when you have decided that you want to (and can) take a whole market by the scruff of the neck and conquer it. Which brings me nicely to...

The big decision – 'boutique or big one'

As I've said, you can function as a sapling 'boutique' for a long time. Twenty people, really committed to the vision and its realization. Happy customers. A reputation for excellence. It's a very nice way to be in business.

As your reputation builds, good things start happening, such as:

➡ quality people start sending you their CV;

➡ banks and VCs start contacting you, offering loans, money for equity stakes (etc.);

➡ the press ring up for comment on developments in your area;

➡ foreign buyers get in contact with you.

Enjoy these. But don't sit back. This is also a time to start asking yourself whether you should consider further growth.

If your company grows further, its nature will change radically – whether you want it to or not. I guess it's to do with the psychology of how many people one can really know well and trust.

If you grow beyond the sapling stage, you must do so as the result of a **positive decision.**

Beyond 20, the organization of the business *has* to become more bureaucratic. The way you hire people changes, and the way you motivate them changes. You may find yourself needing bigger premises: another culture change. The kind of business done by the company seems to change as well. You need bigger income flows, and can get them. But in getting these, you are probably emerging out of your niche and flexing your muscles to take on all comers. The big players start noticing you, and they don't usually hang out a sign with 'welcome' on it.

And once you have left your niche, it is almost impossible to scuttle back.

If you grow beyond the sapling stage, you must do so as the result of a positive decision. You must accept you are entering a new phase in the life of the business, and plan accordingly.

I have worked with start-ups that drifted beyond saplinghood into a kind of limbo, where they still wanted to operate – and feel – like a boutique, but just couldn't. Old hands started complaining. 'The company isn't like it used to be.' 'Nobody listens to me any longer.'

Newcomers didn't know who everybody in the firm was. The start-ups didn't last long in this state: either they grasped the nettle and went for growth, with all its accompanying costs, or they fell apart.

Moving on can be a painful experience. Big companies are a lot less fun than small ones. There'll be more stress. And ironically, people feel a lot lonelier in them. I think our ancestors did live in little groups, and there is something about life in the small company that resonates with this evolutionary heritage. This vanishes once you go for growth.

Is there any alternative? Well, you can start turning down orders and try to become a rather exclusive boutique. Or you can 'clone' – set up a model of yourself in another country. (This is not the same as growth: the end product is not a great, multinational 'oak' but a series of essentially independent saplings in different countries.) Cloning sounds an easy option but isn't: no two business cultures are the same, and a formula that works wonders in the UK may fail dismally in France or the US. If you must clone, involve local people.

If you go for growth, you should end up with a substantial financial reward: you will work incredibly hard in an environment that is not really your natural one, but hopefully not for more than four or five years, at the end of which you will not need to work again. Or, more likely, you can go back to start-ups again, now safe financially.

It will be one hell of a challenge. Can you really turn it down?

The entrepreneur will have no doubt: they set out to change the world, and this is just another step on the road to achieving that goal. Oh, and they'll get the posh HQ and the media attention, too. The cornerstones should be more thoughtful. There are various questions they have to ask themselves when confronting the 'grow/no grow' dilemma. Five criteria – if you meet these, you have passed another crucial hurdle.

1. The market

You must believe you have the ability to conquer a marketplace. By conquer, I don't mean monopolize, but become a market leader with a market share of about 30 per cent, or at least a fighting number two. This is your objective in the mighty oak stage.

Most mature markets have oddly similar structures. There's a leader, with that 30 per cent share (or thereabouts). There's a number two, with about 25 per cent, locked in battle with the leader (think Pepsi). Player number three specializes more, and has about 10 per cent. Other players occupy niches of various kinds. (There are exceptions, of course – natural monopolies – but not that many. Even Bill Gates has been trying to see off Linux.)

The market you intend to conquer will probably end up in this standard shape – if it doesn't at the moment, this is probably because the market is immature. You must believe you have what it takes to end up in position one, two or three as it matures.

You must believe you have
the **ability** to
conquer
a **marketplace.**

2. Sales

You must have a regular flow of sales, from a wide range of customers. You leapt over another hurdle when you successfully delivered to your first 10 customers, but you are now casting the net even wider.

Sometimes your customers actually ask you to grow. Or beg you to. If they really like the service they get from you, they will want more of it than a mere sapling can provide. In this case, you have very little choice, as if you don't offer them your product on the scale they have started to require, they will be forced to head off and find someone who provides something similar in the way they want it.

3. Organization

You should have an established infrastructure with day-to-day tasks such as payroll, delivery, security, etc. under control.

4. Finance

You should have a healthy credit rating. How much can you borrow?

5. People

This is probably the most important criterion of all. The 20 people who are your business must be crystal-clear about how they feel about making the change.

The best way to ensure a successful transition from sapling to growing oak is to confront the team with the decision a long time before it happens, when your staff level gets to 14 or 15. 'Some time in the future, we'll be faced with this choice. What do you think about it?' That way, when the crunch time comes, they'll be clear about which way they want to jump. And that's what you need: 20 clear decisions.

OK, if everyone apart from you says 'no', you've got a problem. If the five founders are divided, you've got a problem. But the most likely outcome is that most of the tribe will be up for it. Those who aren't convinced are not to be banished, not to be airbrushed like Trotsky from Soviet pictures. The growing company is developing a mythology, and anyone who was one of the original 'dream team' has an inalienable and permanent place in that mythology. Give them jobs that feel as much like sapling jobs as possible, jobs without much line responsibility, jobs such as selling into new, exotic markets or running the skunkworks.

Those who are up for the change must brace themselves for a revolution in work style. They are about to become managers in an organization that is colder, more bureaucratic.

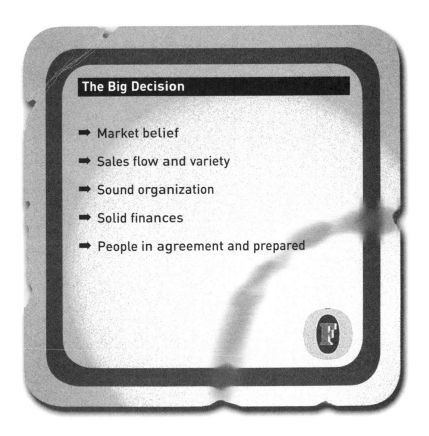

The Big Decision

➡ Market belief

➡ Sales flow and variety

➡ Sound organization

➡ Solid finances

➡ People in agreement and prepared

When you decide to change, draw up a new business plan. This plan, which I call your market conquest plan, is like the business plans that crossed my desk at the launch network every day – only it's real. Real sales, real markets, real targets that you actually expect to meet. There are plenty of websites offering template business plans (www.morebusiness.com and www.e-start.com are recommended) – now is the time to use them.

Drawing up a market conquest plan is the ideal way to end your time as a sapling. You should feel in your bones that the plan is workable – you really do understand the market, you really do know your potential customers.

The tribe is about to move off the savannah into the first towns.

Life will never be the same again.

Life will never be the same again.

the

mighty

oak

This is the next phase of your business's life. It begins when you pass the magic number of 20 in the team: the entrepreneur, four cornerstones and 15 'dream-team' players.

There may well be semi-critical change points beyond entering the 21-person 'oak' stage, at 5,000 employees or 100,000 or some other such figure, but I do not believe they are as important as the two great changes, from seedling to sapling and from sapling to oak. This is because once the business is in the oak stage, it requires formal, bureaucratic management. This remains true from then on, whether you have 30 employees or 300,000. If this view seems rather lopsided – well, I'm writing from an entrepreneurial perspective.

Consider astrophysics: the universe was apparently formed in a 'Big Bang' and the first few moments were when the really amazing changes took place. After that, the universe just kept on expanding.

If you have enjoyed the book so far, you may not believe you are cut out for life in the oak. All those rules and conventions are what you joined a tiny 'Big Bang' business to get away from! Your belief about this may not be right. Some people make the change with ease. They are sharp enough to see the change coming, and they treat it as a whole new adventure. 'Right! Now I'm going to learn how to be a corporate manager!'

Others are wise enough to know they won't enjoy this, and retreat to the sidelines and hire specialist managers. If they do this, they must let these people manage, and not meddle, committing the error of 'getting a dog and barking themselves'.

As with most changes, the worst option is to ignore the change to oak and pretend things are going to muddle along as before, really...

Whichever option they take, the oak stage will be a time of reflection for entrepreneur, cornerstones and dream team alike. Before, they all knew what they were in business for. They did it for the buzz, for the challenge, for the tribal adventure. But now...

OK, they're going to make shed-loads of money, but that was never their number one motive anyway. In the bigger 'oak' organization, those tribal joys have gone, and money looms ever larger. Salaries are bigger, as are expense accounts, and for entrepreneur and cornerstones,

The worst option is to **ignore** the change to oak and **pretend** things are going to **muddle along** as before, really...

a giant cheque is appearing on the horizon if they decide to go down particular 'exit routes'.

I talk more about exits later, but now a brief overview of 'oak' life is needed. It will be very much briefer than my comments about seedling and sapling enterprises because most management books are about oak organizations. They don't say *everything* about this kind of business, however.

Culture, people

One thing remains constant, at least – business is still essentially about people. But just as your dream-team players were different from your four fellow founders, you will be recruiting different sorts of individuals into the growing oak. You will have a different, more distant relationship with them, too.

You are now taking on *employees*, people who are unlikely to feel that much loyalty to the company. They are selling you their skills at the market rate. So buy those skills, treat the vendors fairly, and don't expect the kind of commitment you got from the sapling dream team.

Employees' motivational hierarchy will be different to the one I discussed in the last chapter, or rather the section of the hierarchy that you still see will be different. They will probably meet their higher needs outside work, or if they do try to do so at work, it will be via a career that will take them off to another company once they have achieved what they wanted with you. Those low-level things like money and conditions will matter more.

How do you find these people? The method of hiring I recommended in the last chapter – using contacts, then introducing them to everyone in the team before you take them on (and giving everyone a veto) – will cease working once you outgrow the sapling phase. This is partially because the company is just getting too damn big, but also because of the kind of people you are taking on.

When you get beyond about 50 employees, you will need an HR department. Its director will set up and run formal structures for recruitment, promotion and training, as well as handling the mechanics of payroll, pensions and so on. They will write a 'company handbook' that reiterates the mission statement of the company and sets out policies on issues such as equal opportunity, disciplinary proceedings and other formal processes like how to claim expenses.

Your own role in the company will change, too. You are no longer captain of the team, but a director of a large business. Directing a large business is very different from sports captaincy. It's less about flair and humanity, more about rules. Less about motivation, more about strategy.

Now is the time to read those management books that talk of business in military terms: big companies are like armies, and their clash is like a war. Step forward two paces, Clausewitz and Sun Zi.

You are not quite as visible as you used to be, though you still have to stay positive – remember the story about Next – and occasionally have to put on a big, crowd-pleasing show.

New cornerstones

As I have said, many cornerstones and dream-team players (and some entrepreneurs) don't feel at home in the corporate world. Or they do feel at home, so much so that they keep working at the rate they did in the first years of the company and begin to show signs of serious stress: cornerstone burn-out.

Either way, they must be replaced, permanently.

Note that this replacement is *operational:* their place in the *mythology* of the company must remain intact. If a cornerstone wants (or burns) out, keep them as an unsalaried 'founder director'. Insist they take a long, and long-dreamt-of, holiday or a year out to write that thriller they always talked about (you know, the one about a serial killer in a small software business). When they return, create a leftfield corporate role for them. If they're techies, start a skunkworks. Who knows, they might be like Steve Jobs and turn round and save the company – twice!

No, finding a good enough replacement is not easy. But it has to be done. Your mentor is a great place to start. They are bound to know some quality people with experience of managing big businesses. Note how the mentor remains important even at this stage. Top sportspeople often keep coaches long after they have achieved more than the coach ever did. They know that 'you never stop learning', and that part of learning is to have an excellent teacher. So keep your mentor on board!

If your mentor can't come up with anyone, try your own contacts.

Headhunters are a last resort. They cost a lot and in my experience often present you with a list of people who look good on paper but aren't actually right. If you do find yourself using headhunters, make sure they don't start acting unethically and stealing people from your rivals. I know this advice may sound goody-goody, but this kind of practice is quietly corrosive to your running of an ethical, effective business, and to the kind of morale and loyalty such a business uniquely commands. You might win a few points in the short term, but it is a loser's strategy over time.

Note that if someone tries that on you, it's a signal that a) you're not managing well enough to keep key staff loyal or b) the oppo are getting a bit desperate.

Killing the king

The most difficult person to replace is the entrepreneur, but if you go for growth, it nearly always has to be done some time. Just as parents never really quite see their children as adults – especially when you bring a new partner to meet them and they start telling that story of the time you peed in the paddling pool aged four – in their heart, the entrepreneur is still king or queen of the dynamic seedling, ready to conquer the world with their Beermat Plan.

The kind of leadership that got them this far really isn't appropriate any longer, and the cracks nearly always start to show. Examples: they start building a 'praetorian guard', a clique of people loyal to them, not to the company. The guard start doing things in direct contravention to company policy. The entrepreneur's public behaviour becomes erratic, towards customers or employees.

I'm sure everyone can cite examples of model entrepreneurs who haven't done this, but I have seen it happen so often that you must be prepared for it. It's important not to be judgemental at this time: the entrepreneur is under huge stress. But they are handling it dysfunctionally and they must be removed from operational responsibility or they will drag the business down.

It is, of course, the cornerstones' job to do this, and it is probably one of the hardest things they will ever do. By far the best way is for all four cornerstones to go off-site with the entrepreneur and *persuade* them that the best thing for everyone would be for them to move on.

There is no simple way of doing this, but the following hints might be useful.

➡ Try to see things from the entrepreneur's point of view. What are their issues, their problems? How can 'moving on' be presented to them as a solution to these issues and problems?

➡ Don't threaten them. That creates instant conflict and defensiveness. Yes, you have the boardroom power, but don't flaunt it.

➡ Don't just comment negatively. The more you can frame the discussion in a positive context – 'Look how far we've come in 10 years' – the better. The 'but...' will still hurt, of course, but less than a simple diet of rejection.

➡ Comment on specific behaviours, rather than making a blanket criticism of them as a person. The more the entrepreneur 'takes it personally', the more defensive they will become. Of course they will take it personally, but your job is to *minimize* this reaction. You should know them well enough to know when they are going into 'hurt child' mode. Have you said something badly? Stop the conversation at this point and remind them you are not having a hate session aimed at them but trying to solve a problem.

➡ Stay in control of yourself. Don't allow yourself to have a hate session aimed at them. You probably want to after what the entrepreneur has been up to recently, but now is not the time. If they start getting personal with you, don't go down that road. They're upset, remember. Whatever they say, don't hold it against them.

➡ The entrepreneur must save face. Have a 'golden escape route' ready for them. ('Our CEO is moving on to concentrate on strategic issues as our new president.') Use your knowledge of them, and your imagination, to design a route which would really appeal to them.

➡ Be united. Agree among the four of you what the outcomes of the discussion must be.

➡ Be firm on these outcomes, but have other areas of discussion where the entrepreneur can negotiate *and win*.

None of the above are magic formulae, however. This won't be easy or fun. But it's a lot less miserable than a simple show of boardroom voting power and the inevitable backlash. Companies have been

Try to see things from the
entrepreneur's
point of view.

destroyed by former leaders who have been insensitively disposed of and who then seek revenge.

If you are the entrepreneur in this situation, go gracefully, while at the same time negotiating the best possible outcome for yourself. Part of you will feel deeply hurt, but don't let that part take over and start a war with the rest of the team. You'll probably feel an overpowering temptation to do something really spiteful to the company and those bastards who have turned round and stabbed you in the back. Resist it.

How do you express your anger normally? An electric guitar? Whacking hell out of a helpless white golf ball? The written word? If you don't think it's too absurd, go and see a counsellor and rant and rave at them. *Don't* let your rage loose in your family home or in your business practice. But don't just lug it around with you, either.

Get negotiating! Once the negotiations are over, make a 'clean break', during which you treat yourself to something you've always wanted to do but never had time for.

Give yourself time to get over what amounts to a personal loss, almost like the loss of a loved one. The natural process of grief involves denial, anger, bargaining and, finally, acceptance.

Accept what you have achieved. You have changed the world. You have provided for yourself and your family a standard of living unimaginable to most people on the planet, and beyond the reach of 99 per cent of your fellow countrymen.

Accept that this change was inevitable. Few entrepreneurs make the change from beermat to corporate boardroom wholly successfully. There is no shame attached to having to go when the time is right.

Remember the old adage that 'the best revenge is a happy life'. Get yourself back in balance, enjoying life.

Meanwhile, back at the business, the entrepreneur has to be replaced. This is the time to find an industry professional skilled in the operation of a big company. They will bring in new ideas. The company's learning and growth process continues.

As with finding cornerstones, talk to the mentor first and use personal contacts if possible.

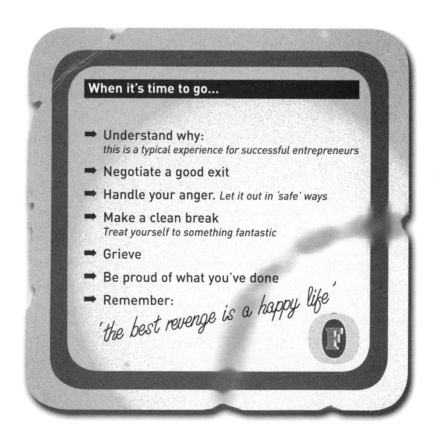

Other aspects

Looking at the various other aspects of 'oak' business, rather than just trying to replicate what the management textbooks tell you, I will just make a few observations.

Sales

The sales department was God in the sapling phase, but now it begins to lose its power as marketing becomes important. The firm will appoint a marketing director (and if they are wise, put them on the board). Sales and marketing directors should be of equal rank, something the sales cornerstone may find hard to stomach. But stomach it they must.

As in all areas of the growing oak, the sales department itself becomes more bureaucratized and less fun.

Note that *advertising* now has value, as you are aiming at a broader market. *PR*, in effect free advertising, is of value too.

Systems

Systems become a major issue everywhere. In seedling and sapling companies, the best form of communication was personal contact, plus the odd e-mail or memo. Now communication needs to become formal. As does finance, and, well, everything else, really. In seedling, and even sapling, companies you probably got by with Word, Excel, memory, and pen and paper. Now you need to develop systematic, formal ways of doing things.

When you are sure of these systematic, formal procedures, yield to one of those people who have been trying to sell you an IT system for the last three years, and *computerize* the procedures. Note that the system must be flexible enough to deal with a manyfold increase in personnel, as that is what you are aiming for.

Finance

The finance cornerstone will probably find themselves swamped by the management accounts of a 100-person company. Get a big-company finance director on board.

As regards funding, now that you are big and growing, you are in a much better position to talk to VCs. Their risk in providing capital for you is much less than it was at the start, so you can negotiate tough terms with them – terms that keep post-adolescent clever-clogs non-execs off your board, and which keep most of the equity where it belongs, in the hands of the people doing the work.

Law

I still don't think you should take on lawyers full-time because the basic principle of 'don't litigate, negotiate' remains constant whatever size your company is. But clearly the more business you do, the more legal issues are likely to arise. You may need to look for a bigger firm to advise you, especially when you start doing business overseas. If so, be prepared for even more outrageous bills.

Globalization

Don't race into the global marketplace. It's tougher than it looks. Despite a veneer of similarity (McDonald's in Beijing, Kenyan kids in Nike baseball caps), the world's markets are all very different. So many companies have blundered into overseas markets, assuming that if they do it like they do at home plus a few tricks learned off the locals they'll crack it, and have lost serious money. Please don't throw away all that hard work you've put in by opening 17 offices round the world simultaneously.

Don't race into
the global marketplace.
It's **tougher** than it looks.

My tip on going international is 'let the market choose you'. If you suddenly start getting orders from Germany, have a go at the German market. If you secure one big client in an overseas market, set up a tiny office there to service that client, and quietly see what other business you can build up while you're there.

We did 'go international' in The Instruction Set, but only after a great deal of interest from the States. Our US subsidiary was included in the deal when we sold the company but later did a management buy-out, and I'm delighted to say it is still running.

Heading for the exit

Most entrepreneurs and cornerstones take their businesses into the oak stage with some kind of subsequent exit in mind. It keeps them going in what is essentially an alien environment. 'We'll put up with this big business stuff for three years, then we'll be big enough to get taken over or go public.'

This is what we did at The Instruction Set. Actually, I got to quite enjoy the big business world and would have been OK to carry on building a private company. But we got to a point where we had to decide either to compete with some very big players indeed or sell out to one of them. This crisis point was reached at about the time that stock markets were beginning to look overheated, and when an offer came our way, it was irresistible.

All five of us became very rich – real money, not the theoretical stuff – very quickly, but there was plenty of downside.

Despite the reality of life in the 'oak' world, we had managed to keep some semblance of tribal culture in the business, even at 150 people. This vanished the instant we sold out. We had already had to negotiate about our employees behind their backs. And then, one day we had to tell them the outcome of those negotiations. 'Guess what, everyone, you've been sold.' People were in tears. A week after the sale, I'd have happily torn up my seven-figure cheque and gone back to how things were.

I'm glad I didn't, though. The money is nice, but just as important, the sale worked. The new buyer – Hoskyns, now part of CAP Gemini – proved a good place for our people. Many are still there, in senior positions. Others left, then founded their own businesses. One of the most moving days of my life was when, years after the sale, I was invited to a reunion by former Instruction Set employees.

There is usually a compelling commercial logic to trade sales. Most markets begin fragmented, with lots of small players, then begin to coalesce into mature markets, with fewer but bigger players, plus a few tiddlers surviving in niches. *You cannot buck this trend*. You have three options: grow to be a major player, get swallowed up by a major player, or lurk in a niche. The only other option is faff around, see your business poached by growing competitors and go bust.

Initial public offerings (IPOs) are the other major form of exit – going public, on the stock exchange – though they are a lot less common than they used to be, thanks to the dot-com bubble. They sound wonderful – all that money, and all that media profile, too! – but behind this glittering surface lurk horrible disadvantages.

You have **three** options: **grow** to be a major player, get **swallowed** up by a major player, or **lurk** **in a niche.**

One is that a sizeable chunk (around 8 per cent in the UK, over 10 per cent in the US) of all the value you have carefully built up vanishes into the pockets of City institutions. Take a walk round the City and look at the premises these people occupy if you aren't sure whether they overcharge for their services.

Another is the people you suddenly have breathing down your neck. City institutions make even VCs look relaxed and 'long-termist': fund managers get a roasting if their portfolio underperforms for a quarter. You are also public property in a media sense.

Listing on any exchange tends to involve the company in a web of unfamiliar legal, accounting and reporting rules that do it – and its already hard-pressed staff – no favours.

Share prices are volatile, and their movements are often unrelated to your performance. General levels of market enthusiasm rise and fall, as does the fashionability of sectors. Just because the City has decided that widgets are bad business, you're suddenly at the mercy of all kinds of 'corporate raiders'.

And finally, you don't even get to see that wonderful paper wealth you were credited with the day you IPO'd. There are legal requirements about how long you hold stock for – and even when these are satisfied, if you start selling you can set off a market slide. And if the share price has fallen in the meantime…

So what about other exit options? A 'private sale' means being bought by a VC. You can probably guess my views on the desirability of that, though if you've been through the mill of stock market listing, you might collapse into the arms of a VC offering a 'public to private' deal and be quite happy.

But why exit at all? Why not just stay private? This option is in my view the ideal one. Not because it makes you mega-rich, but because private companies can concentrate on what really matters – pleasing their customers – without having to dance to the tune of fund managers or big corporate owners. If you think the stock market is the inevitable end for all businesses, ask massive, world-class and still private companies such as Mars, Virgin, Bechtel, Levi Strauss, Gulf Oil…

Of course what really matters for your business is not what I think but that the team in charge have thought about the matter and have agreed on their preferred route out. You cannot afford to have disunity on this issue. The best way to avoid disunity is to discuss exit early on in the oak stage and to keep revisiting the topic, not to refuel greed but to ensure everyone knows where they are going. 'So we get big: what then?'

Winning for real

What then, indeed?

Maybe you've got a cheque for £1 million (or more) in your wallet. You've won!

No.

Competing is often a lot easier than really winning. The pop world is full of people who can't handle success, and there are plenty of examples in business, too. I worked with one entrepreneur who later went down a spiral of degeneration ending in death.

This spiral had two strands to it, ironically like the two spiralling strands that create life. One was simple ostentation, beginning with the Ferrari in the business car park. The other was abuse of personal power: like all entrepreneurs he was manipulative, but he began to get a kick out of pushing people around. Just how far can you make people jump for money? This soon extended to the sexual area. Allegations of rape were made, then suddenly dropped. At the same time, the consumption mania turned inwards, to drugs. Eventually the police got wind of this and searched his house. Crack cocaine was found, allegedly enough for the police to charge him for dealing. He ended up taking two other people for a spin in his latest car and smashing it into a tree. Nobody survived.

That's an extreme story, but it happens to be true (and well documented in various media articles, just in case anyone thinks I'm overdramatizing).

Winning is about gaining wealth and power, and about handling the consequences, about not letting them take away your common sense and common kindness.

A myth often propagated by the rich but stupid is that they earned their money by solo effort. One against all, Darwinian man. I doubt this is good Darwinism: our ancestors were group animals, not lone hunters like Jaguars or eagles. It certainly isn't a good philosophy of business. Who helped you get where you have got? Have they shared in the success, too? Winning is about ensuring that the people who helped you win have got something out of the win as well.

Competing
is a lot easier
than really winning.

The most obvious examples are your fellow founders – but you should all have huge cheques from the sale/IPO or be getting healthy dividends from your private company, so they are not a problem. What about the dream team? They, too, should be in senior positions within a growing organization, so should be happy they teamed up with you. And the people who joined the spreading oak, employees number 21 to 150? It was these people's reaction to The Instruction Set trade sale that upset me the most, and I was hugely relieved when most of them quickly adapted to the change and prospered in their new, bigger organization.

I believe in a 'points' system, whereby staff gain points in a pool. This pool can be translated into money on realization of the business's value, by ensuring that a tranche of the proceeds goes straight into the pool. This pool is totally transparent – everyone knows what you have to do to get points, and how many points they and everyone else have got. A working example: if the long-serving receptionist has 1,500 points and there are 40,000 points in the pool, and the company sells for £10 million and the rule is that 20 per cent of the proceeds will go to 'point holders', the receptionist will get £75,000.

The vehicle for this would be stock options, not old-style but under the new Enterprise Management Incentive, which allows for up to £3 million to be distributed to staff in a way that is very tax effective.

What if you stay private? You can still give people shares in the company, but they are less obviously of value – who decides what they are really worth? A generous bonus scheme is probably more appropriate here.

Winning is also about 'a good night's sleep', about knowing that you haven't stamped on people's faces on the way up. All through this book I have stressed the value of fair, open, ethical dealings with people – with employees, with competition. I believe there is real commercial payoff to this way of doing business, but it also has the benefit of keeping your conscience intact.

I also believe that being a winner means putting something back. Spread some good karma. It doesn't have to be actively philanthropic, though if you feel motivated to do this, brilliant. My own way of doing this was to create a '70s revival band – in one sense, a complete self-indulgence, but I made sure the band was top class, and I've had people come up to me after gigs and say they've just had the best evening ever. The band was set up to entertain, not to 'make money', and it showed. It never really did make money: profits just got ploughed back into horn sections, light shows, etc., thus creating work for musicians (who could then go off and

Creating

'win-win' situations

is what it has been about all along,

from that very first sale.

create great art if they felt like it) and providing extra entertainment for audiences. And an extra ego boost for me, of course. But that's the point – the situation was 'win-win', like all good business practice.

If you'd like to know more about my alter ego, Confused Disco Legend and 70s Fashion Guru Mike Fab-Gere, you can find him at www.fabgere.com He has been known to accompany me to corporate events.

Photo: Rankin

Creating 'win-win' situations is what it has been about all along, from that very first sale. There used to be a kind of 'castor-oil' morality in Britain: if something hurt, it was good for you. In business it led people to put up with appalling customer relations and industrial relations. In the 21st century, neither of these is acceptable. We have to put effort into creating and developing 'win-win' situations, not just look after number one and enjoy a good whinge when someone gets one over on us.

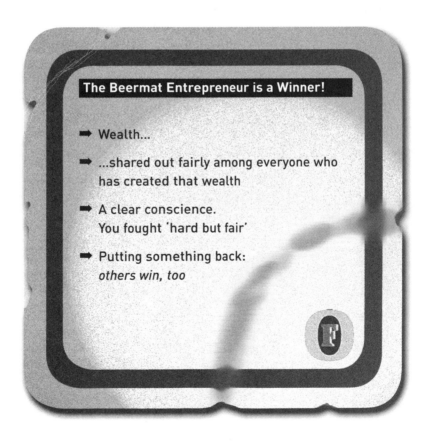

The Beermat Entrepreneur is a Winner!

→ Wealth...

→ ...shared out fairly among everyone who has created that wealth

→ A clear conscience.
You fought 'hard but fair'

→ Putting something back:
others win, too

I wish you every success in your business career. Contrary to what you read in the press, now is a fine time to get a business going. The dot-com boom is over; in this more realistic environment, people who have good ideas, and who go about commercializing them in the right way, can end up with great businesses. You can settle back and really enjoy the journey and, I hope, the fruits of success.

Perhaps my favourite entrepreneur story is of a friend with whom I spent many hours sitting in a particular pub talking about various business plans. He eventually founded a software company and made a lot of money out of it. We lost contact, but a while ago I got in touch with him and he suggested meeting at that same old pub. We did, and half way through a delicious meal, I commented on how much nicer the old place was. The food and drink were excellent, and best of all there was a friendly, convivial atmosphere.

'It's improved a lot since I bought it,' he explained.

'It's improved a lot since I bought it,' he explained.

Appendix A

Turning a good idea into a great business: the hurdles

Τhis is not a list of 'things to do' but a list of points at which it is sensible to ratchet up your confidence in an idea's ability to truly make it.

1. The idea sounds special the first time it is mentioned – in the pub.
2. It still sounds great next morning.
3. It sounds even better when some initial work has been done on it.
4. An experienced business person agrees to champion it.
5. Your first customer writes you a cheque.
6. A founding team of five able individuals commit themselves to realizing the idea.
7. Your first customer is pleased by what the idea has delivered.
8. Ten more customers found.
9. Ten customers delighted by what the idea has delivered.
10. You pass the Five Tests (page 110): market belief, sales, flow, sound organization, solid finances, people, ready and eager.
11. You achieve, fairly, the domestic market share aimed for in your market conquest plan.
12. World domination!

Appendix B
The Instruction Set story

Much of this has already appeared in various places in the text, but here's the whole story from beginning to end.

It begins at the University of Bradford in the late 1970s. I was a chemical engineering undergraduate with an unhealthy interest in the theatre. Though some people unwisely cast me in their plays (usually as a cameo comedy figure), I began to write and perform my own smutty revues. I'd always wanted to perform at the Edinburgh Fringe, but after the university's financially unsuccessful venture in 1979, in true entrepreneurial style and with the blessing of the students' union I took my own show up in 1980 and made a small profit.

The technical director was the BBC-trained Mike Banahan, who although only in his late twenties was a lecturer in computer science. He had written one of the first books on the Unix operating system with another lecturer, Andy Rutter (who drove the van to Edinburgh).

In 1982 I was in the oil and construction business, which was becoming more and more difficult – I was selling a range of services, mainly scaffolding, and becoming more and more miserable.

Mike Banahan suggested I get a job with an outfit for which he had done some freelance lecturing in London, a division of a computer recruitment company. I found myself selling training, and discovered that Mike's expertise – Unix and the C programming language – was much in demand, so all I really had to do was take orders. The envious recruitment consultants nicknamed me 'Keith Prowse'.

I persuaded Mike to join full-time and Andy Rutter did some freelance work. Then one of the people who had been on Andy's MSc course, Pete Griffiths, called in looking for some London-based work – he had fallen in love and decided to move down from Leeds. Pete, the entrepreneur, was the one who immediately realized that we had the basis of a business of our own, and introduced us to his brother, Dave Griffiths, then a VP at Goldman Sachs.

Three of us (Pete Griffiths, Mike Banahan and myself) started The Instruction Set in January 1984, in a basement kindly provided by a company called Quantime. The first morning I sold £20K worth of training, and we were away. Andy joined six months later and Dave Griffiths the following year.

Our business was initially training, then consultancy and software development. We experimented with products, but decided to concentrate on services. Training was never less than 65 per cent of our business.

From very early on, Mike, Andy and I concentrated on what we did best – in their case technical work, in mine sales. Pete (CEO) and Dave (COO) ran the company day-to-day – we had formal input only at monthly shareholders' meetings. We employed some excellent managers: Sally Riley (administration), Nigel Martin (technical), Rick Medlock (finance) and Simon Hawken (sales) amongst others.

We had an initial £30K overdraft, of which we used only £20K. This was guaranteed on our houses, but this only really meant something to Dave, who had the biggest exposure (expensive property and children)! After 18 months the personal guarantees went, and we had a serious celebration.

We were profitable every quarter except one, when we made a big investment in new training materials. We never had any external capital.

In 1988 Rick Medlock and I opened up our US operation in Boston. When I came back in 1989, Pete and Dave told me we had some people who wanted to buy the business. Up till then we had been selling to the industry – now we were getting major end users asking us to deliver major projects, some bigger in scale than our entire turnover. Clearly we had to partner, so we talked to the usual suspects. They all wanted to buy us outright.

We had a choice – take investment, pick a vertical market and compete with the big boys or find a good technical and cultural match and sell out to them.

We joined the Hoskyns Group plc (now Cap Gemini Ernst & Young) in 1989. At that point we had 150 people in the UK and US. Thanks to Pete and Dave, we got an excellent valuation, which we split equally. Pete and Dave took senior positions in Hoskyns, Pete running marketing and Dave one of the systems integration divisions. I was the first to leave in 1991.

Mike Banahan now runs a successful consultancy in Bradford, GBDirect (www.gbdirect.co.uk). Pete and Dave Griffiths are successful Hollywood scriptwriters and executive producers. One of their films is due for imminent release, starring Tommy Lee Jones and Benicio Del Toro. Andy Rutter has done a number of technical consulting roles, including some time with me at RiverSoft.

Ten years after the sale to Hoskyns, former employees organized a reunion, and invited the founding team. There were about 50 people there. It was a very special moment.

Appendix C
The Prince's Trust

The Prince's Trust offers funding and support for young entrepreneurs (as well as other kinds of practical help for young people). Included in the support is a mentoring scheme – the best in the country. Every successful applicant gets a mentor, an experienced business person from their area. If you've got this far in the book, you'll know how important I know mentoring to be.

You need to be between 18 and 30 and unemployed, or underemployed and of limited means (in other words in a lousy, part-time job). The Trust is also committed to helping young people from minority ethnic communities, people with disabilities and ex-offenders.

The Trust has an outreach scheme. You should be able to find a leaflet at your local Jobcentre. Your local bank, when they turned down your loan application, may have pointed you in The Trust's direction (in which case they did you some good, after all). Your local Business Link or Enterprise Agency (useful organizations in their own right) should have information. But if not, you can simply contact The Trust, and they will take a very proactive approach to you and your business. The easiest way to get in touch is via their website www.princes-trust.org.uk. If you can't get access to a computer (are things that bad?), there's a free 0800 number (0800 842842) which will get you through to your local Trust office.

After your initial contact, The Trust make much of the running. Your local Business Development Manager will contact you to arrange a one-to-one meeting and explain what The Trust has to offer and how it works. Essentially, they will help you develop a business plan, which you will then submit to a panel of volunteers (this process is usually pretty informal). If the panel think you and your idea have got what it takes, The Trust can offer:

➡ Loans (and grants in exceptional circumstances)

➡ Mentoring (see above)

➡ An excellent Business Support package, including the opportunity to network with other entrepreneurs.

The Trust have a positive, unpatronising approach. If you think you will be eligible, get in touch with them.

Enjoyed this book?

The Beermat Entrepreneurs are available to speak at functions, to moderate conferences or to carry out mentoring, 'Enterprise Audits' or consultancy for businesses of all sizes.

- Are you keen to introduce more entrepreneurial attitudes and practices into your existing business?

- Are you starting up a business?

- Have you started up a business and are encountering difficulties?

- Do you want a top class speaker for this years' sales conference? (or a great seventies band for the party afterwards?)

If so, we'd love to work with you. We want all our readers and customers to win!

Contact Mike on mike@beermatentrepreneur.com

www.beermatentrepreneur.com